# Smart Choice Cleaning's: Your Carpet and Floor Care Guide

## How to Keep Your Carpets and Floors Looking Beautiful and Healthy for Twice As Long

By John Alzubi

Smart Choice Cleaning's: Your Carpet And Floor Care Guide

Copyright © 2017 by John Alzubi and Smart Choice Cleaning

All rights reserved. No part of this book may be reproduced or transmitted in any form or by any means without written permission of the author.

# Table of Contents

Introduction ................................................................... 1

## Section One: Why, When, and How to Clean Carpets and Floors ................................................. 7

Why Clean? ................................................................... 9

How Often Should I Clean? ..................................... 17

What Method Is Best? ............................................... 23

## Section Two: Choosing A Carpet Cleaner You Can Trust ........................................................ 31

Hiring the Wrong Company ..................................... 33

Why Hiring the Cheapest Carpet Cleaning Company Is Usually a Bad Mistake ................................................ 39

Why a Cheap Carpet Cleaning Company Cannot Provide Good Service ............................................................. 47

Buyer Beware: Bait & Switch Schemes and How to Avoid Them ........................................................................... 53

How To Choose A Reputable Carpet Cleaning Company . 61

The Pitfalls Of DIY Carpet Cleaning ....................... 67

Tile & Grout Cleaning: Why You Should Leave It To The Pros ............................................................................. 73

## Section Three: Your Carpet, Flooring, And Lifestyle ................................................................... 79

How to Choose the Best Carpet for Your Lifestyle ............. 81

How to Choose the Best Floors for Your Lifestyle ............. 89

## Section Four: DIY Tips On Removing Spots, Spills, and Stains .................................................. 101

   Food and Beverage Spills ........................................... 103

   Oil-Based Spills ........................................................... 109

   Pet Stains ...................................................................... 115

   Paint Spills ................................................................... 119

   Spot Dyeing .................................................................. 127

## Section Five: Area Rugs ........................................ 131

   Area Rugs – Are They The Same As Carpet? ............. 133

## Section Six: Water Damage Restoration ............. 143

   Wet Carpets And Floors – Oh, My! ........................... 145

   Conclusion ................................................................... 155

   About the Author ........................................................ 159

## Introduction

The comforting feel of your carpet on your feet lends a sense of warmth to your home. Do you remember those days stretched out on the floor with your loved ones, playing games or just relaxing? The right carpeting adds a comfort and softness to your experience that no other flooring can match.

When you think back on these events, you do not see spots and stains on your carpet - this just doesn't fit the mold of a great experience in your home.

How does your carpet look now?

It is easy to buy great looking stuff; it is a bit harder to keep it that way. If your carpet has been through the natural lifestyle of most flooring, then you are in need of professional help to keep it looking new and inviting. However, many carpet cleaning companies take their clients to the cleaners rather than cleaning their carpets.

This guide is all about helping you find an excellent carpet cleaning company among the scam artists and the exaggerators. You should not have to deal with wet carpet and unprofessional in home personnel. I know a good cleaning company when I see one, and I can help you identify that company in your area as well.

Who am I? I am a cleaning industry professional with over 13 years of experience. I am a Master Cleaning Technician certified by the Institute of Inspection Cleaning and Restoration Certification (IICRC). I have published many articles in the industry as a customer advocate.

I have also served as a quality advocate, helping other cleaning businesses improve and creating more successful relationships between clients and businesses.

Most importantly, I have cleaned thousands of carpets. However, even my happiest customers have had a complaint: It had taken too long to find me! Client after client had either been duped by scam companies or otherwise been so frustrated that they started to clean their carpets and rugs DIY style.

If you have just bought new carpet, this guide will help you avoid the trial and error drudgery of bad carpet cleaners. If you have experienced the problems of trying to find a great carpet cleaning company, this guide has been created to move you away from those mistakes into success with your cleaning company. Here is a sample of what you can expect:

First of all, you will learn the basics of what it takes to clean a carpet properly. We will go over how often your carpet should be cleaned and the best methodologies for cleaning carpets. You can use this information as an initial vet when you begin to interview professional cleaning companies.

Next, you will learn why hiring the cheapest carpet cleaning company is usually a big mistake. You will learn exactly why cheap companies cannot provide excellent service. You also find out how some companies who are looking to cut corners will bait and switch you into paying for much less than you receive.

You will learn how to identify a professional carpet cleaning company. As an advocate for quality in business, I have dedicated my career to locating and uplifting carpet cleaning businesses that want to create good relationships with clients through excellent service. I will give you the ability to see these companies through my eyes, giving you the same ability to identify the best company for you.

I will also teach you about tile and grout cleaning, along with do-it-yourself tips for spots, spills, and stains. If you experience a small accident in between cleanings (we all do), this is essential information for you to have. You will not be doing the professional's job for him; however, you will be helping to preserve the overall look and feel of your carpet until the professional can come in and restore it to that next level. You will learn what to do for food and beverage spills, oil-based spills, paint stains and even pet problems.

Imagine what you will be able to do with a professional opinion on how to choose the best carpet for your lifestyle. That perfect look is within your reach – I look forward to helping you find it. You also learn what to do with wet carpets and floors to preserve them until you can call your professional and have them cleaned.

I look forward to sharing my over 13 years of experience in the business with you. Let's get started!

Section One:

# Why, When, and How to Clean Carpets and Floors

## Why Clean?

You vacuum regularly. You are diligent about cleaning every spot and spill as soon as it occurs. However, did you know that no matter how clean your carpet and floors may appear, they could still be dirty?

In fact, your carpet could look clean and still be holding up to 10 pounds of dry soil in just one square foot – and that is not including the standard mites, bacteria, dead skin cells, mold and other creepy crawlies that lurk in an otherwise "clean-looking" carpet. Not to mention, tile flooring can harbor all kinds of unwanted dirt and grime in surface pores and grout lines.

**That is why your carpets and floors need regular cleaning.**

Would you ever dream of not washing your clothing for weeks on end, or of only changing the sheets on your bed every two years or when unsightly stains cover them up?

Of course, not.

Just like your clothing and bedding, your carpet is made of fabric and needs to be cleaned regularly – not just to make it more beautiful, but for health reasons as well.

The truth is, like all fabrics, carpeting is porous and absorbent and holds onto moisture, debris, stains, and odors.

In fact, the U.S. EPA (Environmental Protection Agency) recommends that the carpeting in your home be cleaned once every 1 – 2 years to maintain a healthy and hygienic indoor environment. Carpet manufacturers suggest the same even if your carpet does not appear to be dirty. Likewise, your tile flooring should be cleaned regularly to remove bacteria, stains, and grime.

**But, why do carpets and floors get so dirty?**

75% of homeowners do not remove their shoes when entering their home, meaning that whatever you have walked through outside is tracked indoors onto your carpeting and tile. Whether it is pollen from the garden, dirt from the sidewalk, oil from the driveway or anything unpleasant you have stepped in outdoors, it gets tracked onto your carpets and tiles.

Additionally, when you cook, airborne oils from your kitchen eventually land on your flooring. Add to these inadvertent spills of liquids and other accidents that add to the hazards your floors are exposed to, and it is easy to understand why your carpets and floors get so dirty.

Even cleaning can cause your floors to become dirty -- the most common cause of dirty tiles and discolored grout is infrequent cleaning and dirty mop water. Instead of cleaning the tile, using a dirty mop and dirty mop water just distributes the dirt from the tile into the grout lines, and spot-cleaning carpets can spread soil and stains if not taken care of properly.

The good news is that there are several significant benefits to having clean carpets and floors.

## Benefit #1 – Appearance

Obviously, aesthetics are one of the biggest benefits of having clean floors. It would be hard to find anything more off-putting than a dirty or stained carpet or floor. It is likely you would automatically have a negative assumption about a person or business if faced with an unsightly floor. First impressions are important. When friends or relatives visit your home, or visitors come to your office or company, the condition of the premises makes an impact.

Keeping your carpet and tiles clean and well-maintained through professional floor cleaning services will not just improve the look of your tile or carpet, but also improve the appearance of your home or office as a whole, making a more positive impression on visitors, clients and employees. A clean and visually appealing floor is welcoming and reassuring and can go a long way toward creating the first impression you are after.

In fact, real estate professionals will tell you that when selling your home or commercial property, that along with a fresh coat of paint, clean flooring and carpeting is one of the first things a potential buyer will notice. If your carpeting is stained or worn, the majority of prospective buyers will mentally make the note "Needs work."

Regardless of whether your property has multiple upgrades, soiled carpets will bring down the perceived value of those improvements.

On the other hand, flooring that looks clean and like-new will lend the impression that your property is "move-in-ready," which will lead to a faster sale and higher selling price.

Additionally, few things will turn a buyer off quicker than odors, which brings us to the second biggest benefit of clean carpets and floors.

**Benefit #2 – Eliminates Odors**
Dealing with pet odors is a major issue for many homeowners with carpeting.

Even the best-behaved pet can have accidents, and between tracking in dirt, shedding, and oil from fur, they can do a number on your floors. Pet accidents are difficult to remove – even when they look visibly clean, they can leave an odor that builds with time.

Lingering odors can be embarrassing when you have company over, but they can also impact your health as well. Pet dander and proteins found in urine can not only create unpleasant odors but can also trigger asthma, allergies, bronchitis and respiratory infections. The ammonia in cat urine can cause health issues such as dizziness, headaches, pneumonia and bronchitis. That is why we list odor removal as the second biggest benefit to clean carpets and floors.

## Benefit #3 – Longevity

Keeping your flooring clean and well-maintained will extend its lifespan, so you do not have to pay for expensive carpet and tile replacement (at least, not anytime soon). By keeping your flooring clean, you increase its longevity. Moreover, since your flooring is a significant investment, it makes sense to take care of it and make it last as long as possible.

## Benefit #4 – Your Health

Regular cleaning of your carpets and tiles improves the cleanliness and hygienic aspects of your home or business. Keeping your flooring clean removes contaminants, outdoor pollutants, and bacteria while eliminating dust mites, soil, and food particles that can affect your indoor air quality negatively, giving you the peace of mind that potential allergy triggers stay at bay.

## Benefit #5 – Maintains Your Warranty

Carpeting is a major investment. Most carpet manufacturers have specific warranty requirements concerning their care and maintenance, and many will honor their warranty guarantees only when carpets are cleaned professionally using specific techniques, products and methods that are in line with their requirements. Using incorrect methods or failing to have them regularly cleaned by carpet cleaning professionals can often invalidate your warranty.

The point is that relying on experts for proper carpet and floor care maintenance is necessary to keep your carpets and floors looking their best, lasting their longest, and staying their healthiest.

How often you need professional carpet and floor care, however, is another question altogether.

## How Often Should I Clean?

Dirty carpeting is not just unsightly. It is packed with dirt and dust particles, oil, allergens, pollutants, and grime. Dirty particles act like sandpaper underfoot breaking down carpet fibers whenever you walk on them. Over time the fibers become crushed and matted holding in even more dirt at the base which shortens its lifespan. If you take good care of your carpet, it will look more attractive and last longer.

Just as you would not avoid scheduling routine maintenance on your automobile by getting it serviced only when the engine begins to make noises, to get the most life out of your carpet it is important to have your carpet cleaned regularly – before it starts showing wear and tear.

## How often should you have your carpeting professionally cleaned?

For the most part, how often you have your carpeting professionally cleaned will depend on how much traffic it gets, and whose feet (or paws) are providing the traffic. Some households can sport clean carpets for up to two years, while others may need to get them cleaned every six months.

By regularly vacuuming and taking care of drips and spills as they happen (using the tips revealed later on in this guide), you can extend the life of your carpet significantly. However, careful maintenance will not eliminate the need to have your carpeting professionally cleaned.

Various factors dictate how often you should have your carpet cleaned. The type of fiber. How old it is. How light the color is. How much foot traffic it endures. Because of this, it is best to use the following guidelines based on your situation to help you determine when to schedule your carpet cleaning.

## Your Carpet Manufacturer's Recommendation

If you have newer carpeting that is under warranty, check your paperwork to find out what type of cleaning is required, and how often. While most carpet manufacturers require that you have your carpet professionally cleaned once every six to 12 months, if you live alone or with another adult and are gentle on your carpet, it is possible you could go up to 16 months between professional cleanings. Check your paperwork to be sure.

## Households with Kids

Between playtime on the floor, everyday spills and accidents, dirty shoes, and increased carpet traffic, kids can truly inflict heavy wear and tear on carpets. If you have children in your home, we recommend the maximum suggested amount of time between professional carpet cleanings should be no more than six months to a year or an average of once every nine months. More active families that have a lot of child guests or indoor/outdoor play may need their flooring cleaned more often.

## Households with Pets

Because pets spend more time on your carpeting than the human inhabitants, they can pose a unique challenge in keeping your floors clean. The combination of fur, dander, dirt and oil can lead to dingy-looking high-traffic areas or areas where they frequently sleep. Pets with bladder or urine issues compound the problem. To fight pet-related carpet soiling, vacuum daily, spot-clean any accidents, and have them professionally cleaned every 6 to 12 months. If you have a combination of children and pets in your home, it may be necessary to have high-traffic areas cleaned more often.

**Households with Allergies or Asthma**

Keeping your carpeting clean is essential for asthma and allergy sufferers. Dust mites, pollen, dander and other particles can get trapped in carpet fibers and exacerbate breathing issues. To reduce allergens and asthma triggers, vacuum your carpets daily with an HEPA-filtered vacuum and have your carpeting cleaned professionally as often as every six months with a hypo-allergenic cleaner, and when spot-cleaning, ensure that the carpet and pad are fully dry because mold or mildew in the pad can trigger allergic reactions.

**How should you care for your carpets between professional cleanings?**

Most home experts recommend that you vacuum your carpets at least two times a week in low-traffic areas, and more often in high-traffic areas. Carpeting industry guidelines suggest that it is best to vacuum carpets once per week in high-traffic areas with a Carpet and Rug Institute (CRI) certified vacuum for each person living in the home. Moreover, if your household includes dogs over 20 pounds, count each of them as a person as well. Before it gets ground in, whenever you see visible dirt or debris on the surface, take care to vacuum immediately. Likewise, attend to spills, drips, and stains promptly, before they sink into the carpet base. Gently blot any stains with a clean, absorbent towel, and resist the urge to scrub. Clean stubborn stains with a cleaner formulated for carpeting, then rinse and dry thoroughly.

## What Method Is Best?

When it comes to cleaning your carpet, one size does not fit all. Just as there are different types of carpet fiber construction and materials, such as shag or Berber, synthetic or natural, there are a variety of cleaning methods best suited for each.

Each carpet cleaning method has distinct advantages and disadvantages – knowing which one is the most appropriate for your particular carpeting is your carpet cleaning expert's job. When discussing how to approach your carpet cleaning needs, here's what you need to know about the pros and cons of each cleaning method.

## Dry Cleaning

Dry carpet cleaning has quickly become one of the most popular methods of cleaning for both residential and commercial carpeting. Dry cleaning involves applying specific powdered cleaning products and specialist machines to clean carpeting with no moisture added.

One of the biggest benefits of dry cleaning carpets is that it does not waste water, and there is no risk of water damage to your carpeting or other furnishings. The method saves lots of time. Wet carpet cleaning needs approximately 24 hours to dry, and cannot be subjected to foot traffic during that period. With dry cleaning, the carpets in your home or business are ready to be used immediately, which makes it a popular choice for commercial applications. Unlike wet methods of cleaning, there is no risk of mold or mildew from carpeting that harbors moisture. It can take as little as 20 minutes before the carpeting can be put back into service.

Unlike some other methods, it is impossible to deep clean carpeting with the dry cleaning process. It can also cause excessive dust build-up inside your home or business, and the powder can become trapped in carpets with a thick plush pile, leading to build-up over time.

The dry cleaning method is best for carpets that can't have any moisture applied to them at all.

**Foam Cleaning**

Dry foam carpet cleaning involves applying a cleaning agent to the carpet. A cleaning machine then whips it into foam consisting of about 10% liquid and 90% air. A brush works the foam into the carpet pile, coating each fiber and suspending dirt and debris. Once the foam dries, the carpet is vacuumed thoroughly, removing crystals of dirt that have been left behind.

Because the moisture content is low, there is little danger of over-saturation, and your carpeting dries fast. It is easy to clean a large area in a short amount of time and doesn't require extensive technical training to accomplish, however, dry foam cleaning is only able to remove an average amount of soiling and staining.

The machines may not provide a very high level of extraction, leaving behind excessive residue which will attract dust and lead to quicker re-soiling. It does not provide high heat cleaning, and there is no soil extraction from deep within the carpeting, so it best used for light maintenance.

**Bonnet Cleaning**

Typically used for light maintenance, bonnet cleaning can also be used for routine carpet cleaning. A chemical solution is applied to the carpet with a sprayer and allowed to dwell for a suitable reaction time. An absorbent pad is then affixed to a rotary floor machine, which then spins over the carpet surface, causing the solution to penetrate the fibers and then pull the soil out.

The advantages of this method include quick cleaning, less wicking, and a rapid drying time.

Bonnet cleaning may cause fiber damage, pile distortion and swirl marks if done by an improperly trained technician. It can also grind soil into the carpet and abrade the surface. Bonnet cleaning only cleans the surface of the carpeting while soil and stains may remain lurking under what appears to be a clean carpet and is, therefore, most suitable for lightly soiled carpets.

**Hot Water Extraction**

While steam cleaning machines do use hot water, they do not clean carpets with steam. Instead, the carpet cleaning machine sprays a cleaning agent or detergent onto your carpeting (acidic for natural fiber carpets like wool and alkaline for synthetics), and then the hot water activates it. Then the bulk of the liquid is extracted with a wet-vac.

The hot water extraction process is typically effective at removing soil, stains and most of the cleaning solution and leaves only a little residue on the carpet. If you have asthma or allergies, there are non-toxic and hypo-allergenic cleaning solutions available that are free of dyes and perfumes when using this method as well.

Because of the volume of water injected into the base of the carpet fiber, it can affect deeply embedded soil, and create wicking and spill stain reappearance issues if executed by the wrong cleaning company. The carpeting must be thoroughly rinsed to remove the pre-spray and eliminate re-soiling.

Also, if done by an ethical carpet cleaning company this method is the most recommended by carpet manufacturers.

## Encapsulation

Encapsulation carpet cleaning provides a deeper cleanthan vacuuming but is less disruptive than hot water extraction. Encapsulation cleaning involves applying an encapsulation solution to the carpet, then scrubbing with a cleaning machine. During the scrubbing, the soil embedded in fibers is released into the encapsulation solution. After the carpeting dries, a vacuum is used to remove the encapsulated soil.

The good thing about encapsulation is it is easy to quickly clean large commercial areas with limited wicking and reoccurring spill stain issues. Encapsulation cleaning dries fast so the carpet can be exposed to foot traffic sooner. Some polymeric encapsulation detergents can even remove detergent residues left in carpeting from previous cleanings. Biodegradable cleaning solutions are also available, and it is effective at removing most stains.

The only downside is that it may be more expensive than other methods of carpet cleaning and, like all of the more modern cleaning methods needs to be performed correctly to be effective.

**Shampooing**
Shampoo cleaning has been the go-to option for a long time – more carpets have been cleaned by the shampoo method than any other over the years, providing a safe, reliable and efficient way to remove stains from millions of carpets. Shampoo cleaning uses a rotary floor machine that has shower feed brushes and is equipped with solution tanks. A shampoo solution is applied to the carpeting and then scrubbed.

Shampooing is a relatively economical system. It provides great agitation which results in deep cleaning and overall delivers excellent results. Additionally, there is a longer dwell time of the cleaning chemicals on the fiber than other methods, such as bonnet cleaning, and a wide variety of cleaning agents can be used to target particular soils or fibers.

To avoid over-wetting and pile distortion, a high level of technician skill is required. Due to lack of rinsing, the residue can build up on carpet fibers, resulting in carpets that re-soil faster. In recent years shampooing has been traded in for extraction or encapsulation as the favored method by most professional carpet cleaning companies.

## Which Is The Best Cleaning Method For Your Carpet?

Now that you know more about the variety of carpet cleaning methods available, how do you choose which one is the best method for your carpet? That is a decision best left to the experts. It is essential to find an experienced, professional carpet cleaning company that is familiar with all of the different types of cleaning methods as they will be able to advise you on which method (or multiple methods) will be the most useful for your carpeting type and material to achieve the best results.

Section Two:

**Choosing A Carpet Cleaner You Can Trust**

## Hiring the Wrong Company

Whether you are a homeowner or commercial business operator, it is easy to forget what an investment your flooring is until you have to replace it.

How well your flooring stands up over time depends on several variables, but with proper care and maintenance, it is possible to ensure your carpet or tile holds up well and looks good seven, ten, twelve or even 20 years down the line.

Cleaning spills promptly, frequent vacuuming or sweeping, and sometimes just luck can extend the life of your flooring – it all depends on how well you care for your carpet, natural stone or tile. Moreover, much of that depends on whom you rely on to clean it.

Regular cleaning by a team of high-quality commercial carpet cleaning and floor care specialists can potentially add years to your flooring, while a sub-standard company can shave years off its life, significantly reducing your return on the investment. Choosing the wrong floor cleaning service can cause headaches and potential damage. Here are some key reasons why:

### Reason #01 – Substandard Equipment

Reputable floor cleaning companies invest in high-quality, powerful, newer equipment. Older, poor quality equipment can affect how well your floor is (or is not) cleaned. It might initially look good, but signs that it has not been cleaned properly will soon show after the technicians have left. Substandard equipment can result in:

- Your carpeting or tile looking worse
- Improper floor cleaning
- Water left that damages carpet fibers and padding or water seeping into or under tiles and grout
- A chemical residue left behind which attracts dirt and soiling

- Damp conditions which encourage microbial growth such as mold and mildew
- Stains quickly reappearing
- And more

**Reason #02 – Lack of Technician Training**

Unskilled, new and inexperienced technicians can wreak havoc on your floors. They are not qualified to use specialized equipment properly, which can result in damage to your carpet, tile, stone or furnishings. They could use the wrong chemicals, or the wrong cleaning method for your carpeting type, or can scratch and chip hard surface floors. Additionally, not knowing how to use equipment properly can result in injury to you, someone in your home or business, or themselves.

**Reason #03 – Incorrect Cleaning Method**

There is no "best way" to clean carpeting – different carpets need different methods based on their fiber type, age, and application. Depending on what kind of carpeting you have, using the wrong cleaning method can cause damage to your carpet. For example, dry methods can cause yellowing in some carpet materials, while over wetting during extraction can degrade and cause delamination issues in others. Using the incorrect cleaning for your carpet type can invalidate your warranty, as well.

**Reason #04 – Damage from Wrong Cleaning Agents**

As I said, there are many different cleaning chemicals designed for various types of flooring. And they all react differently to the flooring material they come in contact with. Over time, using the incorrect cleaning agents frequently can result in irreversible damage. For example, using cleaning products with a high alkaline level or optical brighteners on the wrong carpet material can cause yellowing, fading, and discoloration. Likewise, using the wrong cleaning agents can damage stone and tile floors, too.

**Reason #05 – Expensive Repairs or Replacement**

Damage caused to your flooring by substandard cleaning companies is often irreversible. You will likely be left with the cost of carpet repairs or replacement, which isn't cheap. For example, over wetting during cleaning can cause shrinkage or leave baggy wrinkles. Stretching and re-tacking it can run from $150-$250 for a 200 square foot room. Tears or holes resulting from sub-par equipment can cost about $100 to plug or patch, and replacing an entire carpet typically averages from $2-$4 per square foot. Don't forget about the charge for disposal of the old carpet!

How can you avoid the potential issues, damage, and headaches of dealing with the wrong carpet or floor cleaning company?

In most cases, it is as simple as avoiding cheap carpet cleaning companies that offer "too good to be true" prices. Finding an experienced, honest and reputable floor cleaning company is not always easy, but it is worth the effort. And sometimes, finding a reliable company starts with knowing who not to trust.

# Why Hiring the Cheapest Carpet Cleaning Company Is Usually a Bad Mistake

For most homeowners, saving money is usually a top priority, which is why it is often tempting to make the mistake of hiring a carpet cleaning company offering cheap services rather than an honest, reputable firm that charges appropriately. While there are some situations where a homeowner can reasonably cut corners on products or services, carpet cleaning is not one of them. In fact, when it comes to carpet and floor care, bringing in a cut-rate cleaning crew could cause more harm than good.

One of the biggest problems with cheap carpet cleaning companies is that the industry is unregulated. Since there are no prerequisites – all an unethical person needs to do is come up with a nominal business license fee (typically under $40), scrounge up some cheap equipment, and they can print business cards and advertise themselves as a carpet cleaning company. In many cases, it would be better not to have your carpeting cleaned at all than to hire the cheapest carpet cleaning company in town. Here's why (you may recognize a few of these reasons from the last chapter).

**The "Bait And Switch" Game**

Problems with cheap carpet cleaning companies can start well before the actual work begins. While you might have been drawn in by slick advertisements and discount coupons, it is rare that it is the price you will end up being quoted. They will bait you with an attractive offer, but once you bite, they will begin tacking on hidden fees, upcharges, and extra costs. A typical bait and switch tactic would be to offer a set price per room, and later claim that closets or a hallway are considered rooms. Alternatively, perhaps, they will offer to clean your entire home for a ridiculously low price, but once you're committed, state that standard necessities such as cleaning chemicals are not included. Pressuring you to spend more money than the advertised price is a common tactic. We will talk more about bait and switch and how to avoid the companies that do it in a separate chapter.

## Lack of Regulations

The carpet cleaning industry, other than having basic OSHA requirements about the disposal of wastewater, is a largely unregulated industry. While a basic business license is sometimes required, there are no stipulations requiring liability insurance to protect your property, to provide workman's compensation, or to have properly trained technicians.

This can lead to the perfect trifecta of disaster if you or the technician is injured on your property while they are cleaning your carpets, or if they cause damage to your home. Additionally, they are not required to perform background checks on their employees.

## Improperly Trained Technicians

Training, education, certification, and membership to professional carpet cleaning associations cost money – money that a cheap carpet cleaning company is not likely to splurge on. On the job experience is important, but it is no replacement for formal training through classes, schools, and certifications. A reputable cleaning company typically requires hundreds of hours of formal classroom training to develop the skills that enable them to clean properly, be good at their trade, and provide top-notch service. Untrained technicians can wreak havoc on your carpeting, furnishings, and home. As for what kind of training to look for in a professional cleaning company, we will talk more about that in another chapter as well.

**Giving Felons an Invitation into Your Home**

When you choose a company that is not required to perform background checks on their employees, you are putting yourself, your family and your property at risk by allowing them in. In fact, you have no guarantee that the company's owner themselves are not ex-felons. A cheap carpet cleaning company may not be able to afford background checks, or may not be able to afford to hire someone with a clean background. Not having a guarantee that the person cleaning your carpet has a clean history can be dangerous – homeowners and businesses have been burglarized, robbed at gunpoint, and even been the victims of more violent crimes due to hiring the wrong carpet cleaning company.

**Your Carpet May Look Worse After Cleaning**

Many cheap carpet cleaning companies pay their employees through commissions or a flat rate per job. This is an incentive to spend as little time as possible on cleaning your floors to perform more jobs elsewhere that day. In what is known as a "splash and dash" treatment, the technician may skip using a cleaning solution at all, and only leave you with a wet, not spotless carpet. It takes time to properly deep clean carpet and to extract the moisture thoroughly afterward. If the company has outdated equipment, it will not perform well, won't remove the dirt, or will leave a residue from the cleaning agent that will attract dirt and grime quickly. If all the water is not extracted correctly, you could face issues with mold and mildew taking root in your carpet and pad, or it could shrink, stretch, or discolor your carpeting. It is possible that your carpeting could look worse after cleaning. Even if it looks fine immediately, if not done right, it will become apparent soon when stains resurface, or it begins re-soiling right away.

## An Unprofessional, Unsatisfying Experience

It is tempting to hire friendly, personable people to clean your carpets, especially if they are offering an unbelievable bargain. The problem is that bargain carpet cleaning services rarely turn out to be a good deal in the long run. A cheap carpet cleaning company has one primary goal – to get in, and get out quickly with your money. Their profit is based on turning jobs over quickly, so if you find a problem or have an issue after they leave, it is likely that the friendly person you dealt with earlier isn't going to be so accommodating now. In fact, it is possible they will not even take your call. A reputable carpet cleaning company is also friendly and personable, but they value your satisfaction and are willing to work with you before, during and after the fact to ensure that you are happy.

## Minimize Issues by Not Hiring the Cheapest Company

When it comes to avoiding headaches, don't focus on finding the cheapest carpet cleaning company. Instead, look for someone of a higher caliber, who has a good background, impeccable references, and reviews has the latest, most powerful equipment, and is trained to provide a professional outcome. Ideally, you want to select an honest, ethical company who is going to be upfront about their services and processes, and values your satisfaction, which can be difficult to do if you do not know what to look for in a cleaning company.

When your carpet begins to look dingy and shabby with random spills and stains, soiled foot traffic paths from family, friends, and pets, and it's past time to schedule a professional carpet cleaning, it can be easy to forget all of the above and jump on the best sounding price without giving it much thought.

You want your floors spotless, want them cleaned quickly, and want to pay a fair price for the service. Like many homeowners, the price is often your first concern, but it should not be, and we know you know that.

Your carpeting is an expensive investment, and you need a carpet cleaning company that treats them that way. So, while the price is going to be a factor in your decision, the most important thing to look for is an honest, reputable service that provides quality work.

Many carpet cleaning companies offer deals and bargains that appear too good to be true. That is because they are. Unfortunately, many companies are only in it for a "quick buck," don't care about your satisfaction or repeat business, and provide a mediocre job at best. They offer outrageously low prices to attract unsuspecting homeowners, and then either rack the price up with extra services or up charges, or do an appalling job.

# Why a Cheap Carpet Cleaning Company Cannot Provide Good Service

While you want to save money, it is not reasonable for a professional carpet cleaning company to be able to offer to clean your entire house for $99 and still turn a profit – there will be skimping, poor service or even fraud to do so. When you are comparing different priced services, remember that it costs money to run a good business and provide quality work. When it comes to cleaning your carpets, you do not want the company cutting corners, but that is what they will likely do if they offer cheap deals. Here are just some of the reasons that a cheap carpet cleaning company cannot possibly provide excellent service:

## Professional Equipment Is Not Cheap

Reputable carpet cleaning companies rely on professional, high-quality carpet cleaning equipment to work quickly and efficiently while doing a thorough job of getting your carpet spotless. The equipment investment alone can easily run in the $20,000-$40,000 range. If you want the company to use newer, well-maintained, powerful equipment that does a thorough job, that works out to approximately $6 per job.

## Experienced, Trained Technicians Are an Investment

What caliber of employee do you want working in your home? Would you trust your carpets to a technician with no training or experience? Do you think that someone getting paid by commission, per job, or minimum wage will be committed to doing the best possible job? In addition to wages, a reputable company is also responsible for taxes and workman's compensation. A typical room of carpet cleaning can take up to two hours of paid work. Do you want your technician to be skilled and trained? The cost associated with well-trained technicians averages approximately $1 per job.

## Time is Money

Company costs for carpet cleaning do not begin the minute the technician steps into your home. On average, it will take twenty minutes to locate your home and drive there, and an additional 20 minutes to drive back to the office or the next job. That is time that the employee will be paid for, as well as costs for operating the vehicle. According to the I.R.S., an average 22 mile round trip at $.52 per mile will cost $12. To do a thorough job, the technician should be expected to spend at least two hours in your home. After finishing the job, the technician will spend another 20 minutes cleaning the truck and equipment and filling out paperwork.

## Office Support is Crucial

Before the technician ever arrives at your home, you have to call to make an appointment. That requires an office staff to answer the phone, an office, and overhead expenses such as phones and computers. It takes, on average, twenty minutes to schedule an appointment over the phone and then record the pertinent information on a computer. In addition to overhead costs, the office phone and cell phone usage alone adds approximately $2 per job.

## Miscellaneous Expenses

In addition to the costs associated with maintaining efficient equipment and paying for labor, many other expenses are figured into the price of your carpet cleaning.

For example, if you would like some assurance you will be covered if your beautiful carpet is ruined, you will want the company to have liability insurance. That will add about $3 per job.

Using the correct cleaning agents for your particular carpet fiber type is crucial to delivering a clean carpet. Many companies skimp in this area by purchasing the cheapest cleaning agents available or diluting them. On average, to get the proper cleaning agents for your job, expect to add $2 per job.

How did you hear about the company? You likely saw an advertisement in the paper, or on the internet. The typical carpet cleaning company spends approximately $30-60 on advertising to acquire just one new client. What if you have an issue with the quality of the work a cheap carpet cleaning company provides? What if the spots return? You would probably like the company to come out and remedy the problem, but at ridiculously cheap rates, they would not be able to afford to. Which is why cheap carpet cleaning companies rarely offer a guarantee of satisfaction.

**You Get What You Pay For**
How does a company clean five rooms for $99? In a nutshell, they don't. At least, not very well. That is why they often tempt homeowners with discount pricing but then tack on extra services, fees, and surcharges.

While it can be difficult to choose a cleaning company when you do not know what you are looking for, a company that charges low prices is using substandard equipment, skimping on your service or supplies, or they are on their way out of business.

You can avoid the headaches that are bound to occur when using cut-rate services by choosing an honest, reputable, ethical company that guarantees their work and will strive to do everything possible to keep you as a client instead.

## Buyer Beware: Bait & Switch Schemes and How to Avoid Them

You want to keep your house clean, and by now you understand the benefits of using a professional carpet cleaning service. At the same time, you want to get a real deal and not pay more than you have to to have a happy, healthy environment.

Unfortunately, many carpet-cleaning companies are scam artists who employ unethical methods to try to take advantage of homeowners.

You have probably seen glossy, high-end discount coupons featured on internet advertising deals or in your local paper advertising carpet cleaning services at very attractive rates. However, when the sales representative arrives, instead of receiving that cut-rate offer, you find that their estimate is much higher due to hidden upcharges, questionable add-ons, and other fees that weren't included in the initial offer. This is a common scam known as "bait & switch," and it is perpetrated all too frequently by unscrupulous carpet cleaning companies. The following is detailed information about this tactic, to help you recognize bait & switch practices and how to avoid them.

**What Are Bait and Switch Tactics?**
Bait and switch is a dishonest sales tactic used by many companies to pressure a customer into purchasing services they are not interested in or paying more than an advertised deal. When employed by a carpet cleaning company, bait and switch typically involves advertising a particular price and then adding hidden fees until the final cost is much higher. The company "baits" you with a low-cost service, and then "switches" it out in a way that is unfair to you, the customer.

**Here is an example of a typical bait and switch tactic:**

You take a company up on a low-priced offer to clean a room, but once the sales representative arrives, they state that the price does not include costs such as cleaning agents that are essential to clean your carpet properly. Another typical bait and switch tactic is to advertise to clean multiple rooms for one low price, but being informed during your in-home quote that a closet, entryway or hallway constitutes an entire room. It would be similar to advertising an "all-inclusive" vegetable stir fry, but finding out that "all-inclusive" just means vegetables and the noodles or rice they are served on are extra, and use of chopsticks will cost $10.

Many companies use bullying, coercion, and intimidation. For example, recently a Southern California carpet cleaning company was convicted of the practice after numerous customers reported the company for intimidation, bullying, and false statements designed to coerce them to pay more than advertised. According to the Deputy City Attorney Adam Radinsky, they charged elderly customers more than other clients. One 85-year-old Santa Monica victim stated that a company representative demanded $2,000 to clean her 570-square-foot apartment. When she declined, he pressured her and incrementally lowered the bill to $795. Eventually, the woman was so intimidated that she agreed to pay $560.

After the cleaning, her carpeting was left soaking wet for three days, and the company ignored her calls.

## Protecting Yourself Against Shady Bait And Switch Scams

So, how can you protect yourself against these tactics and ensure that you will not be a victim of bait and switching? Here are some red flags that indicate a carpet cleaning company is using underhanded tactics:

**Unbelievably low price.** If a cleaning service offers a price that sounds too good to be true, it most likely is. Quality carpet cleaning detergents, time and labor are all expenses for a carpet cleaning company. If an advertisement offers to clean your carpets for $9.95 per room or your entire home for $69.00, it is not likely the company can do that and turn a profit.

**Quotes are given by the number of rooms**. When a company quotes by the number of "rooms," instead of per square footage, they may later claim that a foyer or linen closet is considered a room. An honest carpet cleaning company will ask for the square footage in advance and quote an accurate price per square foot before they come to your home (or visit your location to be more precise).

**Employees are paid commissions.** If their employee is being paid by commission only, they have an incentive to try to tack on additional charges, features, and products. Your home is "an exception." If the sales representative begins adding extra charges because your carpet is "thicker than usual," your rooms are an odd size, or the stains on your floor need special treatment, they most likely are trying to pad their bill.

**They push a "best cleaning method."** While there is a variety of standard carpet cleaning methods (all of which we covered in an earlier chapter), there is no such thing as a universal "best method." The best method for your specific carpeting will depend on the condition, pile, fiber material, age and amount of cleaning required.

**Pushy salespeople.** If the technician arrives at your home and tries to upsell you for things such as adding Teflon into the cleaning solution or charging extra to deep clean areas that don't need it, they are using hard-sell tactics. Carpet protectants cannot be added to the cleaner (it is a separate process), and you should not be paying for extra cleaning in areas that aren't soiled.

## Questions To Ask a Prospective Carpet Cleaning Company

To get a feel for a company's operations and ensure you do not end up the victim of a bait and switch scam, ask the company the following questions:

**Question 1.** What carpet cleaning techniques do you use? If your carpet is still under warranty, most carpet manufacturers recommend specific types of cleaning methods.

**Question 2.** Do your technicians have specific training to do the job properly?

**Question 3.** Do you pay your employees commission, per job, or are they paid an hourly wage?

**Question 4.** Are there extra charges for travel or fuel surcharges?

**Question 5.** Does the estimate include the cost of the cleaning agents being used?

**Question 6.** Are there any hidden fees, expenses or charges not covered in the estimate?

**Avoiding Bait and Switch Scams**
The best way to avoid becoming the victim of an unethical carpet cleaning scam is to know whom you are

dealing with. Read reviews from previous customers on social media and review sites. Contact the company and ask specific questions about the methods, processes, practices and materials they use. Find out if their technicians are experienced and have specialized training. Ask about their cleaning chemicals and equipment. A reputable, honest cleaning company will welcome answering your questions and giving you a straightforward quote with no hidden catches.

# How To Choose A Reputable Carpet Cleaning Company

Selecting a quality carpet cleaning company takes more effort than just conducting a random Internet search and choosing whoever shows up on the first page of Google, or looking for discount cleaning coupons – you need to do research. All carpet cleaning companies are not equal, so consider the following tips to find the right carpet care experts for your specific needs.

**Do Their Technicians Have Industry Training and Certifications?**

A professional carpet cleaning company will employ technicians who have specialized training in the use of The Carpet and Rug Institute (CRI) certified cleaning products, equipment, and methods. They should hold Carpet Cleaning Technician certification from the IICRC (the Institute of Inspection, Cleaning, and Restoration). Ask what types of training and certifications a company's technicians have received.

**Avoid the Lowest Price Option**
If you have not figured this out by now, you have not read the previous sections of this guide.

While it is understandable to want to save money, when it comes to carpets, the carpet cleaning company with the lowest price may not be the best choice. When cheap companies offer a price that seems too good to be true, it is. Sometimes they offer a cut-rate price just to get a foot in the door, and once inside, they will add services, upsell, or identify other issues to push the price up. Consider recommendations and quality first, and make the price your secondary concern.

**Consider the Carpet Cleaning Method**
There is no one "best" method of cleaning carpeting – every carpet has a technique or process that is best-suited for its type and material, and most require a particular

cleaning method in their warranty. Some cleaning options are steam cleaning or a wet method which requires drying time and some use "dry" treatments that can be walked on immediately. Others use powerful cleaning agents and others only use environmentally friendly cleaning agents (refer to the chapter titled, "What Method Is Best?" to know the differences between each approach and where they are most applicable). Look for a carpet cleaning company that offers the treatment option that works best for your home or business.

**Research Prospective Carpet Cleaning Companies**
It is crucial to investigate prospective carpet cleaning companies before choosing one. Ask your friends and family for recommendations, and check online review sites such as the BBB, Yelp and Angie's List for positive experiences and Google search the company name "+complaints" to weed out companies that have created bad experiences. Once you have identified a couple of prospective companies, ask them for personal references of previous customers who were satisfied with their work. References from carpet retailers, flooring retailers, realtors, and interior designers are a plus.

**What Type of Cleaning Products Do They Use?**
It is important to use the proper cleaning agents for your particular carpet material and type. Using the incorrect

type or one that is too strong or ineffective can result in discoloration, delamination, shrinkage, other damage, or in carpeting that is not clean. If you or one of your family members suffer from chemical sensitivities, ask whether their chemicals are toxic, organic, all natural, hypoallergenic, or eco-friendly as well. Remember that "all-natural" doesn't necessarily mean it is safe. Orange oil, used in many cleansers and deodorants is a 100% natural product, but many people have sensitivities to it or even allergies. Simply ask to be sure.

## Do They Have a Business License and Proper Insurance?

To protect your home, furnishings, and family, working with a licensed and insured company is important. Ask the carpet cleaning company whether they are licensed in your state, or check online at your local government websites, or use Angie's List License Check to determine what licensing the company needs in your area. Don't hesitate to ask for proof of any licenses they claim to carry.

Also, the cleaning company should also carry workman's compensation insurance to protect their worker from any injuries while performing a service on your property, as well as liability insurance to protect your property.

Otherwise, in the case of an accident, event, or damage, you will be paying out of pocket for damage or injuries. At the same time, ask whether the company has vetted their employees by running background checks on them – welcoming ex-felons into your home is never a good idea.

**What Are Their Professional Standards?**

When you choose a carpet cleaning company and schedule for a cleaning service, you expect the technician to be dependable and show up on time. Can they assure you that they will keep their appointments on time? When you call their office, is your call answered promptly? Do they offer a solidly written estimate before they begin cleaning? Moreover, do they guarantee their work, and for how long? An ethical, honest, professional carpet cleaning company cares about customer satisfaction and will offer you a guarantee on their work.

# The Pitfalls Of DIY Carpet Cleaning

You might be encouraged by seeing the carpet cleaning machines available for rent at many grocery stores and home improvement centers, and feel like attempting to undertake a carpet cleaning project yourself, but for most homeowners, it is an ambitious task that is a lot harder than it looks. While your carpet stains may be driving you crazy, resist the urge to tackle the job yourself.

When you are tempted to take efforts into your own hands remember that you are not adequately trained and many things can go wrong (many of the same things you are trying to avoid by not hiring the wrong company).

There are many issues and errors that can occur to your carpet because of incorrect DIY carpet cleaning methods – here's just a handful of examples and reasons why.

**It Is Hard Work**

Deep carpet cleaning is not as simple as vacuuming. It is hard physical labor. The rental machines are hefty and awkward to maneuver, and it takes a long time. In addition to having to move all your heavy furniture and belongings yourself, rather than taking the couple of hours you are imagining, it could drag out to a several-day chore.

**Poor Cleaning Results**

Professional carpet cleaning companies, not surprisingly, have expensive, specialized, van-mounted professional-grade equipment. Rental machines are not anywhere near as powerful. They are designed to be compact and easy to handle. That means they are typically low in power. To get your carpets immaculate, you need to move very hot water quickly through the carpeting fibers, and then suction it back out completely. Most rental machines cannot heat water to the correct temperature or provide robust enough extraction.

**Damp Carpeting Issues**

Deep cleaning requires plenty of water and powerful suction to extract as much moisture as possible, which lightweight carpet cleaning machines just can't handle. It is imperative that your flooring be dried properly to avoid issues such as mold and mildew which can not only discolor and cause shrinkage to your carpeting, but also create a bad odor in your home, and even trigger allergies and asthma. Inadequate drying will occur when you do not have the proper fans or equipment.

**Ruined carpets**

When done incorrectly, a non-expert's carpet cleaning attempt could result in overwetting, which can cause delamination. Delamination causes the wall-to-wall carpet to separate from its backing, leading to unattractive and irreversible wrinkling that cannot be flattened and destroys the finish on your carpet fibers. Additionally, over wetting can result in discoloration and shrinkage.

**Carpeting That Soils Quickly**

You would think that if you put much effort into cleaning your carpet that the clean, fresh look would last quite a while. However, many times an ambitious homeowner will find the opposite is true – your carpet soils again rapidly. Thorough vacuuming and a DIY approach to carpet cleaning do not completely release ground in dirt that is embedded into your carpet fibers which will lead to the quick resurfacing and reappearance of stains you thought you had removed. Also, you may use too much detergent or soap, and not be able to rinse and extract it adequately. Residue left behind from cleaning agents creates a sticky surface that attracts dirt and grime, and could make your carpets look dirty faster.

**Hidden Expenses**
The quality and capability of rented carpet cleaning machines can vary wildly, so rental costs will vary as well, especially when what you thought would be a quick afternoon's work turns into a multiple-day job. However, even if you opt for a higher-end model, remember that some other stranger has used it before you, and it may have been poorly cleaned or of poor condition, which will be reflected in substandard carpet cleaning. You will also have to spring for expensive cleaning solution, which may or may not be appropriate for your particular carpet fibers. If you have heavily stained carpets, you will no doubt also be running back to the store for specialty pre-treating and spot removing products.

**Avoid Headaches by Hiring Professional Carpet Cleaners**
Because you do not clean carpets for a living, it is easy to overlook the pitfalls that come with a DIY carpet cleaning attempt. Over-shampooing and over wetting can

cause severe damage to your carpeting, and frustration with how difficult the effort can be will likely result in doing a poor job that requires calling in experts to complete. Save yourself much time, stress, effort, and unpredictable results by hiring professionals to do the job right from start to finish (and use the tips provided in the previous chapters to hire one).

## Tile & Grout Cleaning: Why You Should Leave It To The Pros

Tile floors are the ultimate combination of form and function, aesthetics and utility. A historically perennial favorite for over 7,000 years, tile flooring was used to pave luxurious Assyrian and Babylonian homes and businesses, yet it is still one of the most popular flooring options in modern building design. Today's affordable tile flooring still offers the same benefits: versatility, longevity, low maintenance, durability and beauty. While floor tiles are relatively easy to clean, they are not indestructible, and using incorrect cleaning methods can damage and compromise your tile floors.

Most tile surfaces are relatively resilient and impermeable, but they can discolor chip and scratch. Grout, due to its porosity, can collect dirt, oils, spills and grime, which can discolor and degrade its integrity. Cleaning spills and daily mopping and sweeping is key to maximizing your tile's lifespan, but it will not reach hidden dirt lurking in the surface or grout lines, and if done incorrectly can damage and compromise your tile floors. Here are some harmful tile cleaning techniques you should avoid to protect your investment:

**Aggressive Cleaning Techniques**
While tile and grout may appear to be impenetrable, they can scratch easily. Any rigorous scrubbing can abrade the surface and cause microscopic scratches. Glazed tiles, in particular, will show wear and tear to their finish from aggressive cleaning, and any grout will suffer from harsh scrubbing techniques. Never use abrasive cleaning brushes or pads, scrubbing powders or steel wool. Instead, use a clean, soft towel or rag to clean the surface gently.

**Using a Floor Vacuum**
It is important to remove dirt and dust from your tile before it can scratch the surface and settle into the grout, but you should never use a floor vacuum to do so. Floor

vacuums have a beater bar designed to remove dirt from a carpet's pile, which can chip tile edges, scratch the tiles, and deteriorate the surface. Also, the wheels can cause damage to delicate tiles. Instead of vacuuming, just use a broom and dustpan.

**Mopping and Air-Drying**
Keeping your tile floors clean is essential to prolonging their beauty. Daily mopping is a good way of doing that, but don't make the common mistake of washing them and letting them air dry. It may look like they are drying quickly, but water could be seeping into pores in the tiles, or absorbing into the grout, which can loosen grout and loosen tiles. Don't allow water to sit; after mopping, dry your floors with a soft towel or rag immediately.

**Using Harsh Chemicals**
Cleaning up spills as they happen is the best way to protect your tile surfaces. When a spill is allowed to sit, or when floors tiles begin to look dingy, it is tempting to reach for a strong chemical cleaner. Resist the urge to use harsh chemicals – using the wrong cleaning agent can cause more damage than the original stain. Different tile surfaces require different cleaning products. For example, chemicals that can be used safely on ceramic tiles will damage marble, granite and other natural stone tiles. Ammonia and bleach are two of the most common

culprits. They may create an immediate difference in appearance, but over time they can cause your tile and grout to bleach, powder or discolor.

**Using a DIY Steam Cleaning Machine**
There are many DIY chores that you can safely do around your home or office, but using a steam cleaning sold in stores is not one of them. The pressure can be too high, causing water vapor to remove the top layer of grout or even entire chunks of grout. These steam cleaning machines can also damage the tile installation and surrounding areas such as baseboards and cabinets. The machines remove the seal on your tiles and grout but don't replace it, leading to a surface that will quickly stain again.

**Not Sealing Grout**
Grout in and of itself is a method to hold tiles together, not to seal the spaces between the tiles. While epoxy grout gives a bit of protection, cement-based grouts are more common and require a sealant to prevent stains from sinking in and repel water, spills, and moisture. Failing to seal your grout will result in a porous grout that attracts and absorbs liquids and stains that cannot be removed. There are two types of grout sealants: penetrating and nonpenetrating. Both need to be removed and reapplied over time. Not sealing your tiles

can result in discolored tiles, and water that sinks into grout can end up causing mold and mildew problems.

## Not Calling In the Professionals

While you may be tempted to bypass using a professional tile cleaning service and take a DIY approach, doing so puts your flooring at risk. Not only is hand-cleaning tile floors yourself messy and uncomfortable, but it is also almost impossible to achieve the results you will get from hiring a professional tile cleaning company – and you can cause damage to them by doing it incorrectly. Only regular professional tile and grout cleaning services that should be performed an average of once every three years can safely and thoroughly clean and restore the luster to your tile floors.

Section Three:

**Your Carpet, Flooring, And Lifestyle**

# How to Choose the Best Carpet for Your Lifestyle

Selecting your new carpeting is a decision that shouldn't be made lightly. While it may be tempting to want what's underfoot based on factors such as color, shade, or price, if you do not match it to your specific lifestyle, you could be setting yourself up for a huge disappointment. The type of lifestyle you lead and the conditions the carpeting will be subjected to should significantly influence your choice. Factors such as how much traffic your space entertains, whether you have pets, or even how much light comes through the windows can have an effect on the longevity and appearance, but how well the material fits your lifestyle based on these factors overall is even more important.

## Finding the Perfect Carpet Fabric for Your Lifestyle: The Pros and Cons

### Nylon

Nylon is one of the most popular carpeting fiber types for residential and commercial applications today. It is highly sought after due to its solid reputation for being durable, attractive, and relatively easy to maintain. Moreover, because it is an exceptionally strong fiber, it stands up well to heavy use and abrasion. In addition to being highly resilient, nylon has good texture retention which allows it to maintain its original appearance.

**Pros:** Nylon holds up well to foot traffic, and reacts well to professional cleaning, so even fibers that have flattened easily bounce back. The carpet fiber is fade-resistant and permanent when the color is solution-dyed.

**Cons:** Because nylon is a very absorbent fiber, it must be protected with a stain protectant to prevent spills from sinking deep into the fibers. Nylon is susceptible to bleach and red dyes, such as Kool-Aid, so it might not be the best choice for households with young children.

### Cost of Nylon Carpeting

Nylon carpeting is more expensive than the other carpet fibers that we will cover except for wool. Its durability makes it perfect for lower grade (entry-level) applications, but it is also appropriate for higher-end, more expensive products. Depending on the application and location, nylon carpeting may be the best value for your dollar.

**Lifestyle Compatibility**
Ideally used in:

- Homes or commercial businesses that receive a lot of foot traffic.
- Homes with pets.

**Polyester**
Polyester is a popular carpet fiber choice due to its glossy appearance, low cost, eco-friendly properties, and high level of stain resistance. Its high-luster appearance results in carpets of beautiful colors.

**Pros:** One of polyester's biggest attractions is its inherent stain resistance, which is almost on par with olefin. It is one of the most eco-friendly synthetic carpet fibers – not only is most polyester carpeting today made from recycled PET plastic soft drink bottles, but the carpeting itself is recyclable. For the best wearability, look for at least a 60-70 ounce weight.

**Cons:** Polyester is not as durable as nylon carpeting, and it mats down more. Furniture can make indentations that are difficult to remove. It can also retain residue from cleaning products or oil from bare feet or pets, causing soiling of the fibers.

## Cost of Polyester Carpeting

Polyester is less expensive than nylon, offers good value for the money, and is a great option for budget-driven renovations. It is available in a vast selection of colors and styles, at almost every price point and quality.

## Lifestyle Compatibility

Ideally used in:

- Applications where you anticipate replacing the carpet in a shorter amount of time.
- Homes with children.

## Olefin

Olefin is a synthetic fiber used to make a variety of products, including carpeting. The generic term for polypropylene, due to its wool-like appearance, Olefin is valued in the carpeting industry and often used in looped Berber styles. Its finish can range from matte low-luster to high sheen.

**Pros:** Olefin's solution-dyed fibers are highly stain-resistant, and it does not react to harsh chemicals like bleach (although, we do not recommend testing this fact as bleach will peel away the backing from your carpet). It is hydrophobic, which means it does not absorb liquid. Because it dries quickly when wet, it does not encourage mold or mildew growth. Also, Olefin is extremely fade-resistant and won't discolor from exposure to sunlight and UV rays.

**Cons:** Olefin fiber is not as resilient as other fibers, and doesn't bounce back as well after being compressed. Because it is oleophilic, it attracts oils that can lead to soiling, and so it is not as suitable for homes with pets or for areas such as kitchens or dining rooms.

### Cost of Olefin Carpets

Olefin fiber carpeting is considerably less expensive than polyester or nylon carpets. However, it generally won't last as long, so the immediate savings may not pan out long-term. Often the lowest price point in commercial or residential carpeting, Olefin is a good solution for renovations where the budget is the primary consideration.

### Lifestyle Compatibility

Ideally used in:

- Lower traffic areas in residential and commercial applications.
- Basements.
- Children's bedrooms and play areas.
- Outdoor patios and sunrooms.

**Wool**

Wool is the most commonly used natural fiber in carpeting. While synthetic fibers are the most popular overall, and wool is more expensive, it has a niche. Wool is naturally resilient and retains its original appearance well. Wool carpeting is very durable and can last for decades when properly maintained.

**Pros:** As a natural fiber, wool stains easily, but does have good resistance to soiling, and resists dirt embedding in the carpet fibers. Unlike synthetic fibers, wool has a natural flame resistance, and will not burn. Due to its natural absorbency, it can act as a humidifier in drier climates. The most durable and most luxurious fiber, when selected for the right lifestyle and properly maintained, wool carpeting can remain beautiful for hundreds of years.

**Cons:** Wool is a high-maintenance fiber that requires more effort to care for than synthetic fibers. Wool, if improperly treated, can shrink, and therefore, must be professionally cleaned. As a natural fiber, it is prone to shedding, vulnerable to bleach, and is less stain resistant than synthetic fibers. Because it is absorbent, it stains easily and is not suitable for areas such as bathrooms, where there is moisture retention.

### Cost of Wool Carpets
Wool is one of the most expensive carpet fibers and typically much pricier than high-end synthetics such as nylon. While there are some affordable entry-level wool carpets, many run upwards of $10-$20 per square foot.

### Lifestyle Compatibility
Ideally used in:

- Homes or offices that are kept immaculate.
- Areas with exposed fireplace hearths.

### Other Considerations When Selecting Carpet
In addition to the carpeting material, other factors should be weighed when choosing a carpet fiber that fits your lifestyle, such as weight, twist, density, quality of underpadding, and warranty. For example, a carpet of polyester fiber with a dense construction and high twist

will outperform a lower density, lower twist nylon carpet. You should examine all of the carpet components above before making your final selection on which fiber is right for you because there are so many variables. Working with a reputable carpet retailer is also key. If you do not know what to look for in choosing a reputable carpet retailer, we give our highest recommendation to those who have generously referred you to this guide.

# How to Choose the Best Floors for Your Lifestyle

Hard flooring, such as tile, has an absolute beauty and aesthetic that works well for many residential and commercial applications. It is typically easy to clean, sleek, and adds visual interest to floors. Unlike carpeting, tile and stone can be cold underfoot, which can be pleasant in warm climates, but chilly during winter months.

Because it is hard, it is best suited for areas where you will be standing for periods of time. Just as in the last chapter we discussed the importance of selecting the right carpeting for your lifestyle, your tile flooring choice deserves the same consideration. The following is information detailing the benefits and drawbacks of some of the most popular flooring options.

**Porcelain**
Porcelain is a highly durable type of ceramic. It is typically harder, stronger, and more water resistant than many other types of tiles, making it a good candidate for a variety of architectural surface covering applications.

**Pros:** Porcelain is a very low-maintenance flooring choice. It has a natural stain and water resistance and can be kept clean by spot cleaning with a damp rag, regular sweeping, and damp mopping. It is non-absorbent, hygienic and easy to disinfect. Porcelain does not burn and can be used to restrict the movement of flames in the event of a fire.

**Cons:** Porcelain tile is hefty. That can make installation a more laborious process, and restrict the use of the product to ground floors unless the building has been built to handle the extra weight and stress.

**Durability**
As one of the toughest flooring options available, porcelain tile is dense, hard, and solid, making it resistant to many large impact stresses. Its density makes it

resistant to liquid spills, staining, and when given a melted glass glaze, is virtually impervious to water.

**Cost of Porcelain Tile**

One of the more expensive tile floorings, porcelain tiles can be somewhat pricey. Also, installation can add 25% - 50% of the total cost. However, when properly installed and maintained, porcelain tile can last for decades, paying off the initial investment over time.

**Lifestyle Compatibility**

- Suitable for a variety of residential and commercial applications.
- It can be used in high-traffic areas and can withstand heavy equipment use in industrial environments.

**Ceramic**

Ceramic flooring is available in a wide variety of colors, shapes, and textures. It is a versatile architectural resource that is suitable for various environments that require water and stain resistance.

**Pros:** Glazed ceramic floor tiles are impervious to water and stain penetration, and naturally resistant to damage from high humidity conditions. They are relatively easy to care for and are easy to clean by wiping or damp mopping.

**Cons:** When unglazed, ceramic tiles look rustic, but need to be sealed, as they are vulnerable to liquids and spills. Their grout lines between tiles also need to be sealed to prevent moisture from seeping between and under tiles to prevent from encouraging the growth of mold and mildew.

### Durability

Ceramic flooring is extremely tough, resilient, and difficult to crack. Properly installed and maintained, ceramic flooring can last for 10 - 20 years and longer, and if a single tile break or crack, it is easy to replace.

### Cost of Ceramic Tile

Ceramic tile is relatively affordable, with most tile flooring running $5 - $10 per square foot, making it more expensive than carpeting, but cheaper than hardwood.

### Lifestyle Compatibility

- Ceramic tile, when sealed properly, is ideal for moist environments such as kitchens or bathrooms.

- Ceramic's durability makes it suitable for a variety of residential and commercial applications.

## Terrazzo

Terrazzo is a unique flooring material created by exposing marble, stone or glass chips on the surface of concrete, which is then polished smooth. While it can be poured as an entire floor, terrazzo tiles are also available, making installation much easier.

**Pros:** Beautiful, elegant, and long-lived, terrazzo flooring is also easy to clean with a damp mop. Terrazzo is a beautiful flooring in contemporary settings and high-end lofts and is well known in the luxury housing market.

**Cons:** Terrazzo is quite slippery and when polished has a slick surface that can cause falls. In commercial settings, it needs to have floor coverings in high-traffic areas or have a grip-coat applied to prevent slipping.

### Durability

One of the most durable flooring options around, due to its concrete reinforcement, it is hard, doesn't crack, is resistant to water and spills, and doesn't stain.

### Cost of Terrazzo Tile

The $9–$50 per square foot price, depending on whether it is tile or a solid poured floor, makes terrazzo flooring one of the most expensive flooring options available.

**Lifestyle Compatibility**

- Because it can be slippery, it may not be an appropriate flooring choice for families with children or elderly members.
- It is a popular choice for commercial and public buildings due to its longevity and ability to be repeatedly refinished.

**Travertine**

A type of natural limestone that forms near mineral spring deposits, travertine is available in a variety of beautiful earth tones such as tan, brown, rust and beige, making it an attractive stone flooring.

**Pros:** Each tile is unique, making any installation using them a one-of-a-kind floor. It is an abundant eco-friendly natural resource that is not only recyclable but also biodegradable. Travertine is solid, strong and durable.

**Cons:** While travertine is strong, it has microscopic pores that can allow liquids and staining agents to seep in. To prevent water damage and staining, they must be coated with a penetrating sealer and topped with a barrier surface sealer, which will need to be reapplied periodically. Travertine tiles are heavy, so they are not suited for second-floor installations.

**Durability**

Travertine can take a beating without showing significant damage from scratches, chips or cracks. While weathering can occur over time, this is often welcomed, as it gives character to the flooring. Polished floors will be more susceptible to scratching, while naturally brush-finished tiles will be more resistant to visible damage.

**Cost of Travertine Tile**

Travertine is somewhat expensive but falls in the mid-range of natural stone options. Its heavy weight may make installation more difficult and more costly.

**Lifestyle Compatibility**

- Depending on how the surface is finished and sealed, Travertine is a good choice for homes, offices and commercial applications.
- As it is an excellent heat conductor, it is popular to be used with radiant below-surface heating systems in bathrooms and other rooms.

## Limestone

Due to its robust nature and durability, limestone is a traditional building and construction material. It is a naturally occurring rock and looks beautiful when installed correctly.

**Pros:** Limestone adds an authentic old world look to any interior. It is available in a variety of natural shades, tones, and textures that work well with decorating styles from rustic to sleek contemporary. Unlike many other natural stone flooring which is cold underfoot, limestone adds warmth to a floor.

**Cons:** Because it is a natural substance, it is very porous and requires periodic sealing to prevent against damage from liquids and spills. While it has a great aesthetic appeal, it requires quite a lot of care and maintenance to prevent staining.

## Durability

Limestone is one of the softer stone products on the market, compared to other natural stones. It is one of the least durable of the natural stones and can chip, crack and scratch easily.

## Cost of Limestone Tile

Limestone is less expensive than many other stone flooring options. While it will be more expensive than porcelain or ceramic tiles, it will cost less than marble or granite.

**Lifestyle Compatibility**

- Best for low-traffic areas.
- In high-traffic areas, it will scratch, chip and break.

**Marble**

Quarried from mountains around the world, marble is one of the most beautiful and sought after natural flooring materials. Prized for lending a sense of style and elegance to interior décor, it has been a favorite in the palaces of kings and queens for centuries.

**Pros:** Marble flooring can instantly elevate the appeal of an interior, giving it a high-end appearance that is hard to imitate. It is available in a wide range of colors and hues, as well as color mixes and veining. Each piece of marble tile used is one of a kind. Marble has a natural translucent property other stone products do not have.

**Cons:** Because it is a relatively soft material, it can easily be scratched, abraded and chipped. It is prone to water penetration, and stains easily. It requires a surface-penetrating sealant as well as an above-surface sealant, which needs to be reapplied annually.

**Durability**

While marble is relatively hard, it is vulnerable to a variety of damages. It has a chemical reaction to acidic substances such as certain foods, beverages, and cleaning products, and once discolored, the staining is permanent. If not installed correctly, marble floor tiles can crack or break.

**Cost of Marble Tile**

Marble falls on the high end of natural stone costs. While it has a shorter lifespan than other natural stone such as granite or slate, it is a premium architectural element that is sought after as an upscale, luxurious flooring option, so is priced accordingly.

**Lifestyle Compatibility**

- Because it can be extremely slick and slippery when polished, marble is not suitable for heavy traffic areas.
- Due to its tendency for staining, it is not an appropriate material for kitchen flooring.

## Granite

A dense natural stone, granite is extremely durable and dependable.

**Pros:** Granite is a beautiful stone that is available in a variety of colors and patterns. The embedded quartz crystals and feldspar give it a sparkle other natural stones do not have and are easy to clean when sealed properly.

**Cons:** It is a heavy material, and is not suited for second-floor installation. Maintenance can be time-consuming, as it is sensitive to spills, stains, and chemicals, and has to be sealed properly for protection.

### Durability

Granite is particularly durable and hard and is largely moisture resistant. However, to prevent unsightly stains, it should be protected with a sealant in moisture-prone rooms.

### Cost of Granite Tile

Granite is a relatively high-end flooring material. Depending on the grade and application, you can expect to pay more than $10 per square foot.

### Lifestyle Compatibility

- Granite is well-suited for kitchens and bathrooms but should be coated with an anti-slip grit in high traffic areas or wet conditions.
- Because it does not fade when exposed to UV light, it is an excellent flooring material for porches, sunrooms, and other rooms that receive direct sunlight.

Section Four:

**DIY Tips On Removing Spots, Spills, and Stains**

## Food and Beverage Spills

It is just a fact of life that no matter how diligent you are, inevitably, a mishap or accident with food or beverages will result in a stain on your carpet.

We have all had situations where a carpet stain is likely to happen. Perhaps your daughter knocks her juice off the table, or you host a great family get-together featuring mixed drinks and bottles of your favorite red wine. Consider yourself lucky if you can get through family celebrations, parties, or even day to day life with kids without encountering a stain on your carpet.

If you do experience a minor spill, don't fret! We have compiled a list below of the most common food and beverage stains homeowners frequently deal with and how to tackle them.

**The First Key Is To Take Action Quickly**

When faced with a carpet stain, it is essential that the spill is addressed immediately. Allowing the spill to sit will let it sink deep into the fibers and make it harder to remove later. For example, leaving a milk spill on your carpet might not cause a visible stain, but it will turn sour and create an unpleasant smell.

**The Second Key Is To Resist The Urge To Grab For Stain Remover**

Resist the urge to pull out a commercially made carpet stain remover such as Resolve. Many homeowners make the mistake of spraying a wet stain with a carpet cleaner and then brushing or scrubbing at the stain. Unfortunately, the process of brushing and scrubbing works the stain into the carpet padding and backing and makes things worse. Not to mention, Resolve itself is a very high residue cleaner, and we have even seen it stain carpets when applied.

The best way to treat food and beverage spills is to use wet vacuum them. By using a wet vac, you are working against gravity to pull the stain out of the carpet. Also known as a shop vac, or portable carpet spot cleaner, they extract the stain rather than spreading it around by scrubbing. Use the wet vacuum to remove the stain and as much moisture as possible, then blot dry with a clean, absorbent cloth.

If you do not have a wet vacuum, place a stack of paper towels on the liquid and set a nonabsorbent weight on top of the towels for an hour or so. The second method will likely press some of the liquid into the backing and pad, so it should not be your first option, but it is much better than scrubbing and spreading the stain.

## Cleaning Specific Stains

All stains are not created equal. Some are greasy. Some have dyes or deep colors that linger in your carpet. For tips on how to approach specific stains, keep the following suggestions in mind.

## Red Wine

It never fails. You are having a party with your friends, and you are all having a very good time, sipping wine and socializing – and then someone inevitably spills red wine on your white carpeting. If you address the spill right away, you can prevent the wine from staining.

If you wait, the wine can act as a dye on your carpet fibers. If the stain is still wet, pour club soda or water over the area and use a wet vac, then blot the stain with a clean, dry cloth. Mix a solution of cold water, a couple of tablespoons of vinegar, and a few drops of dishwashing liquid in a spray bottle to make a spot spray. Spray on the stain and allow to sit. Clean with the wet vac again, and blot to dry.

**Soda Pop and Juice**
When a high-sugar beverage such as soda or juice spills on your carpet, not only can it stain your flooring, but the sugar can attract pests, and because it is sticky, it will attract dirt.

Additionally, many sodas and children's juice drinks contain artificial coloring which acts as a dye, and some juices, such as grape or cranberry are natural fruit dyes. Follow the basic instructions for removing wine stains, but make several passes with the wet vac to ensure that all the residue has been removed

**Coffee and Tea**
Coffee and tea are acidic and have both historically been used as fabric dyes, so it is not surprising that if you leave coffee or tea spills to set on your carpet, they will stain. Tea also contains tannins that can stain as well. How badly it will stain relies heavily on the material of your carpet fibers and how long you allow the stain to sit.

Clean coffee and tea stains quickly. Use a wet vac as soon as possible and remove as much of the liquid as you can. Coffee can be oily, so for stubborn stains, increase the amount of dishwashing liquid in your spot spray. For tea stains, sprinkle some baking soda or borax over the stain and brush with a toothbrush. Let it sit, then clean with the shop vac, and blot to dry.

**Spaghetti Sauce**
Cleaning spaghetti sauce from carpeting requires quick action due to the natural dye in tomatoes, which can leave a permanent red mark. Scrape up the spill with a spatula or spoon to remove as much sauce as possible. Then use paper towels to blot the spill. Continue blotting until the towel stops picking anything up. Mix a half-teaspoon of dishwashing liquid in a cup of warm water and put in a spray bottle. Spray the stain and let it sit for 10 minutes. For stubborn stains, work the solution gently into the fibers with a toothbrush, and then blot gently. Follow up by cleaning with the shop vac and blotting dry.

**Know When to Call In the Experts**
There are some instances when do-it-yourself carpet stain removal techniques just won't work. Instead of turning to harsh chemicals or rough cleaning methods, save yourself a headache and get the stain treated by a professional carpet cleaner. If you have a seriously stubborn food or

beverage stain and are afraid of causing more harm than good to your carpeting, it is time to call in the experts and get the stain removed correctly and permanently (if possible). The sooner you call, the more likely that stain can be eliminated.

# Oil-Based Spills

Oil spills on your carpet can cause the most stubborn, unattractive stains you will ever have to deal with – and they are some of the most common stains homeowners experience. Hazards from oils lurk everywhere. Food mishaps are a common culprit: dropping a serving bowl full of salad dressed with olive oil and vinegar on the dining room carpet, knocking the pizza box face-down on the family room floor, or dropping fried food can all lead to unsightly oils stains. Food is not the only source of oil, however. Do-it-yourself fans can track in motor oil on the bottom of their shoes, and machine oil and oils from asphalt can track onto carpeting as well – even walking barefoot on your carpet can transfer oils from your skin!

## Tackle Oils Spills As They Happen

The worst thing you can do in the event of an oil spill on carpeting is to put off cleaning it up. Oil that is allowed to set on carpeting will embed itself in the fibers and act as a dirt magnet. What started as a seemingly insignificant spill will soon look like a major stain.

## Three-Step Oil Cleanup

Some large oil stains can be tackled by using a wet vacuum to remove the oil, but for most homeowners, the results are not great. With large oil stains, it is best to call in professional carpet cleaners who are best equipped to handle significant spills. For most other oil mishaps, there is a simple three-step process to mopping up oil from carpeting: Remove excess oil, absorb oil, and clean the carpet.

- The first step to combating oil stains is to eliminate as much of the oil from the surface as possible. If the oil has pooled on your carpet surface, use a spoon or spatula to remove the excess. Place clean towels over the affected area and blot the spill to extract as much oil as

possible. Repeat the process until no more oil can be absorbed.
- The second step is to absorb the oil and draw it out of the carpet fibers. Sprinkle an absorbent powder, such as cornstarch or baking soda, over the stain and allow it to set for a few minutes. Brush or vacuum the powder away. Repeat until the powder stops absorbing any oil.
- Finally, clean the soiled area with an appropriate spot cleaner solution. Rinse, or use a wet vacuum to remove any residue, and pat dry with a clean towel.

## Cleaning Methods for Specific Oils

Different types of oils respond differently to different cleaning methods. You will have more success removing an oil stain from your carpeting by using the proper cleaning solution and method. Here are the best ways to handle the most common oil issues on carpets.

## Cooking Oil, Salad Oil, Vegetable Oil Stains

Edible oils are best removed from carpeted floors via a mild, soapy solution. After completing the steps of removing the oil and applying absorbent powder, add ¼ teaspoon of liquid dishwashing detergent to a cup of warm (not hot) water. Apply with a bottle sprayer and let sit for a couple of minutes. Blot with a clean towel and repeat until the cloth no longer picks up oil from the area.

**Car Oil Stains**

For car oil spills, first blot up any surface oil, then sprinkle an absorbent powder over the stain, as in the second step. To clean the stain, mix one tablespoon of ammonia with one cup of water. Dip a clean towel or sponge in the solution and apply it to the dirty area. Don't scrub or grind or you will work the oil into the carpet fibers. Instead, use the towel to wipe the area gently. Follow up by rinsing the spot or using a wet vacuum. Pat dry with a clean cloth.

**Machine Oil Stains**

A commercial nail polish remover containing amyl acetate can be a good cleaning agent for tackling carpet stains from machine oil. Follow the necessary steps for blotting and absorbing the stain, then clean the area with the nail polish remover. Don't pour it on the carpet. Instead, apply it using a white cloth or paper towel. When the stain is gone, remove the amyl acetate residue with a dry solvent.

**Know When to Call a Professional Carpet Cleaner**

While the basic three-step process for cleaning oil blemishes from your carpet work well on almost any type of oil spill, they have their limitations and work best on very isolated, small stains. Follow the basic cleaning guidelines and most small spots will be banished. For stubborn oil stains, or for larger spills, bringing in experts with specialized equipment and know-how will save you a lot of headaches and aggravation.

## Pet Stains

If you have pets in your home, one thing you can count on is accidents on the carpeting. Whether you have a new pup who is working on their housetraining, an elderly dog, or a cat that has marking issues, at some point, you will be dealing with cleaning urine from your carpets. However, there is no need to panic! If you clean your carpets properly, you will be left with fresh smelling carpets, while also discouraging future accidents. Learning how to deal with disasters as they happen will make life much easier for you and your pets.

**What Not To Do**

If you are like most homeowners, your first instinct upon finding a urine spill is to cover it with paper towels and blot it up. Resist this urge! When you press the spill into the carpet, you are working it into the fibers. Likewise, attacking a stain with a spot cleaner does not solve the problem – it dilutes it and spreads it further. Pet urine does not just stain the carpeting, it penetrates the fibers, and the odor will permeate the padding and encourage more accidents. As it dries, the liquid may evaporate, but the urine crystals remain, becoming more concentrated and pungent.

**Clean Stains the Right Way**

Cleaning your carpet the wrong way can not only result in unsightly stains and smells, but it can also encourage your pet to continue soiling that area. When you approach pet accidents correctly, you eliminate those issues. Follow these steps to eliminate immediate stains and discourage future soiling.

**Clean it Now.** The longer you wait to clean the accident, the more difficult it will be to remove. While it might not be convenient, life will be easier if you tackle it now. If you wait, the stain can become permanent in just a few hours, and lead to permanent discoloring, especially with light colored fibers.

**Use the Correct Equipment.** Use a wet vacuum to extract the urine or feces. If you come across a stain that is still damp, it is essential to remove the liquid before diluting it with a spot remover. Use a wet vac, shop vac, or any of the popular handheld models such as Little Devil, Bissell, or Little Green Machine.

**Use the Correct Cleaning Agent.** After you have removed the liquid, apply a low residue spot remover to fresh stains, or an enzyme spot remover for old stains. When using an enzyme cleaner, let it sit for at least 20 minutes or according to the product label instructions. Don't oversaturate the area. Enzymes digest the bacteria that cause the odor in urine and works best for spots that have been sitting for more than a couple of hours. For a homemade solution, mix white vinegar at a 1 to 3 ratio. Don't ever use bleach as it can discolor your carpeting.

**Rinse the Spot.** Use your wet vacuum or carpet-spotting machine with clean water to extract the cleaning solution. The leftover cleaning solution can leave visible stains if you do not remove it. Once you have done all of that - blot the area well with clean, dry towels.

**Stubborn Stains**

Sometimes, even with your best efforts, you are still left with unsightly stains. Often, a spot will become larger and darker as it returns. Alternatively, many spot removers can leave residues that attract further soiling. If this happens, saturate the area with clean water and use the wet vacuum to extract the stain. If it persists, use a different spot-cleaning agent and clean it again. If you notice a slight yellowish discoloration, hydrogen hydroxide can be misted onto the stain, allowed to sit for an hour, and then removed with a wet vacuum.

**Know When to Call In the Professionals**
If your carpet is excessively stained, spot-cleaning may not be the solution. If you are not able to remove pet stains on your own or are dealing with a vast area of soiling, it is probably time to call in the professionals. Carpet cleaning businesses that specialize in stain removal are experienced in dealing with pet issues, and are knowledgeable about all the required tools, cleaning agents and processes that will help you regain your clean, fresh-smelling carpets.

## Paint Spills

There's nothing quite like a fresh coat of paint to liven your walls and bring a room's color palette and décor together. However, while color can transform your walls in a positive way, paint on your carpeting is a major decorating faux pas. There are many ways that paint can end up on your carpet. Perhaps your son got a little too creative while painting his model cars, or maybe those chairs you painted weren't quite dry when you moved them into the living room. Accidents happen!

As professional carpet cleaners, we hear all kinds of stories from customers about how paint spills caused a disaster on their carpeting.

Here's a real scenario that is far too typical:

A client had scheduled to have her carpet cleaned, and when the carpet cleaners came into the home, the carpet was covered with paint spray. They'd just had their walls painted, and when the so-called "professional" painters made a mess on the carpet, they excused the damage flippantly, stating, "It is no problem because you are going to have the carpet cleaned. The carpet cleaning company will be able to remove all the paint".

## Paint on Carpeting is a Special Challenge

It is a common misconception among homeowners that it is easy for professional carpet cleaners to clean paint from carpeting. Unlike typical oil, grease or dirt stains, paint presents a different cleaning challenge. Because carpet is fabric, paint can bond to the fibers, and often (especially if the paint has dried) the only way to fix the stain is to remove that portion of the carpet. The problem for this homeowner was that although some of the paint spills were only hours old, others were left over from work they had done sloppily from weeks before. A professional and ethical carpet cleaner can remove much of the new stains fairly easily, but the older spills are much harder to tackle. In fact, you will be charged more to get it done, and it still won't remove some of the dried-on sprays.

**Timeliness**
When it comes to paint and carpeting, time is of the essence. The sooner you call a professional cleaning company for emergency carpet cleaning, the better the chance that your carpeting can be restored to its previous beauty. Calling immediately, or at least within the first 24 hours, is essential. Even if you have spilled an entire gallon of purple paint, chances are professional cleaners will be able to get rid of the stain. However, waiting just a couple of days can be the difference between having a clean, attractive carpet, and between having to replace it. Timeliness is crucial when it comes to carpet stains like paint. Protect your carpeting as well as you can while you are painting, but if you have spills, fast action is necessary. If we can get to it within a day, we can usually get the paint stains out.

**"Don't Worry, its Water-Based Paint."**
Another common carpet stain misconception is that if paint is water-based, it is easy to clean up, even if it is dried on. We often have to educate homeowners about the composition of water-based paints. While the base is water, it is blended with acrylic or latex. When the paint

dries, and the water evaporates, the acrylic or latex remaining will bond permanently to your carpet fibers just as permanently as the paint bonds to your walls.

**Paint Spill First Aid**

No matter how careful you are while painting your interior or working on a craft project, it is easy to spill paint on your carpet accidentally. If you knock over an entire gallon of paint, remove as much paint as possible without scrubbing. Cover the paint stain with damp towels or plastic to prevent drying, and call a professional carpet cleaning company immediately. While a major spill merits an immediate call for expert help, if a few minor paint mishaps occur, there is a do-it-yourself solution. Spot cleaning any spills quickly can save your carpet's appearance. Remember that if you do tackle paint spot removal, always test any cleaning agents on a portion of carpeting that isn't visible first.

**Removing Water-Based Paint from Carpeting**

- If the paint is still wet, scrape off any paint sitting on the surface with a spatula. Blot the stain with a clean, wet sponge or paper towel and rinse until the paint is removed. Don't scrub or rub vigorously, just blot gently and rinse.

- If the paint is dry, dampen the stain with a clean sponge and allow to sit until the paint begins bleeding. Blot up the paint with a clean, damp towel.

## Removing Water-Based Latex Paint from Carpeting

- If the paint is wet, immediately blot the spill to remove as much of the paint as possible. Use a clean, damp sponge or towel on the surface, and don't scrub; you could push the stain deeper into the fibers.

- If the stain has dried, mix some hot water with a little mild dishwashing detergent and apply with a clean sponge. Work from the outside edges of the spill toward the center, and allow the solution to sit for a few minutes for the paint to soften. Once the paint is soft, continue to apply more of the solution while scraping the surface of the paint with a knife or tailor's pin. Remove the bits of dried paint with a clean, dry towel and then vacuum.

## Removing Water-Based Acrylic Paint from Carpeting

- If the spill is still wet, remove as much of the paint from the surface as possible. Apply glycerin to the stain and allow to sit for a few minutes. Blot with a clean towel. Remove any remaining residue with rubbing alcohol, then clean again with a mild detergent and water solution. Blot dry.
- If the paint is dry, call for help from your professional carpet cleaner.

**Removing Oil-Based Paint from Carpeting**

- If the paint is wet, call for professional carpet cleaning immediately. Don't attempt to use solvents to remove an oil paint stain, as the solvents can damage your carpeting worse.
- If the paint is dry, you might have some success using a steamer to remove the stain. Apply steam directly to the paint while picking at the paint with a tailor's pin or needle. Try to break the paint up and pull it off without damaging the fibers. Small drips may be removed this way, but for larger spills, you will need professional help.

**Call In the Experts ASAP**

Whatever the situation, if you are faced with unsightly paint stains on your carpet, chances are you are going to need help removing them. Professional carpet cleaners have the equipment and know-how to remove a wide variety of paint stains. How satisfactory the stain removal is will depend on how long you wait before you call.

## Spot Dyeing

No matter the type of carpet that you have installed in your home, it is important to take care of it to the best of your ability. However, accidents do happen sometimes, and restoration services will be needed for special situations. Take for instance that you spill fingernail polish remover on your carpet. This type of chemical may take the color away from your carpet. If this happens, you will want to spot dye the carpet. Moreover, while you may be tempted to spot dye the carpet yourself, it is usually best to have a professional company do it for you as it is a very specialized skill.

## What is Spot Dyeing?

Spot dyeing takes place after you have spilled a dye removal chemical on your carpet. The dye removal chemical removes the original color of dye in the carpet, causing it to look blemished. Bleach, strong acids and peroxide are three common types of chemicals that can remove the dye from your carpet. However, spot dyeing is when you add the original color of dye back to your carpet (or get very close).

## Can I Do It Myself?

You can, of course, try to perform spot dyeing yourself using store bought dyes such as Rit, but there is a good chance you will not be able to match the exact color of your carpet. There is a certain technique used in spot dyeing that helps ensure the original color of the carpet is correctly matched and this requires the mixing of colors and having almost perfect knowledge of the color wheel. If you do not have experience in spot dyeing, it is highly recommended that you acquire professional help.

## Why Do We Recommend Bringing In the Professionals?

Professionals in spot dyeing understand the ins-and-outs of mixing colors and applying them to the type of carpet you have in your home. Because of this, they are more likely to help your carpet achieve its original beauty when spot dyeing.

If you have an area of carpet that needs to be spot dyed, we highly recommend that you allow a professional company such as us to perform the spot dyeing process for you.

Section Five:

**Area Rugs**

# Area Rugs – Are They The Same As Carpet?

One of the easiest and best ways to decorate your home or office workspace is with area and oriental rugs. It is important to remember, though, that these two types of rugs do differ in their maintenance and repair work when compared with carpet. If taken care of properly, oriental and area rugs can last for many years, making them a wise investment. Here is an overview of area and oriental rugs, including how they are different from carpet, their advantages, and how to properly clean them.

**What Is An Area Rug and Oriental Rug?**
Area and Oriental rugs are similar to a loose piece of carpet, meaning they are not attached to a wall. These

types of rugs are not glued to the floor, nor are they tacked or nailed down. Not all area rugs are oriental. To the untrained eye, it can be a bit tricky to tell the difference between a machine-made rug and an oriental rug, meaning it has been hand knotted. Oriental rugs are completely hand-knotted and are made of natural materials. Regardless of whether you invest in an oriental rug or an area rug, they need to be cleaned regularly and professionally.

## How are Oriental Rugs Different from Carpet?

Many people view carpet like they do their shoes. Sure, both are nice when you first buy them, but after a bit of wear and tear, it becomes natural to want to replace them with new ones. Oriental rugs, on the other hand, are extremely expensive, meaning you will want to make sure they are properly cleaned and taken care of so that you do not have to replace them. An elegant oriental rug can cost anywhere from three to 20 times or more as much as an area rug because there is an enormous amount of time and craftsmanship invested into making them. Some oriental rugs come with price tags upward of $25,000, and this is for one that fills a standard dining room or living room. So as you can see, the price of an oriental rug makes it all the more necessary to take care of it.

## How Are Area Rugs Different From Carpet in the Way They are Maintained?

The Institute of Inspection, Cleaning, and Restoration Certification explicitly states some rugs should not be cleaned with hot water extraction. Moreover, unlike carpet that can be maintained and cleaned in your home, many area rugs need to be cleaned elsewhere.

For example, if you have a red oriental rug and it is cleaned while laying on your white carpet in your living room, there is a high chance that the dyes from the rug will leak through to your carpet, thus leaving a red dye stain on your carpet.

This is why it is so important to send your rugs to a professional company that specializes in cleaning area rugs.

Another way carpet and area rugs differ in how they are maintained is that area rug cleaning requires someone who has extensive training beyond carpet cleaning and experience in cleaning rugs made of natural materials.

A company worth hiring to clean your rugs will employ workers with proper training, and they will also provide insurance to compensate you for any damage that may occur during the cleaning process.

This helps to ensure you are completely covered from a loss if your rug is not returned to you as you expect.

Area rugs differ from carpet in the way they are maintained. Here is a brief look at four tips you should be following to help ensure your area and oriental rugs are kept properly.

**1.) Move them regularly:** First and foremost, you will want to make sure you move your rugs at least once every one to two years. Ideally, though, rotating them once every two months is even better, especially rugs that are in high traffic areas. Rotating the rugs allows for distributed wear and tear, which leads to a more uniform look, increasing both the appearance and value of your rugs.

**2.) Beware of sunlight:** Please keep in mind that any of your area rugs that are exposed to direct sunlight have the potential of their dye fading. To prevent this fading, you will want to keep them out of direct sunlight as much as possible. This is another reason rotating the rugs on a regular basis is of the utmost importance. The less exposure they get to sunlight, the less fading.

**3.) Don't comb the fringes:** If your area and oriental rugs have fringes on the ends, don't comb them if they become tangled. Instead, you will want to flip the rugs end over end to loosen the tangles. If you comb them, this can lead to the natural fibers in the rugs to become damaged.

**4.) Vacuum regularly:** One of the best ways to extend the longevity of your area rugs is to vacuum them on a regular basis, preferably once a week; this will help the natural fibers from becoming packed down due to high amounts of traffic. Remember, to make sure you avoid putting runs or tears in the fibers of the rugs, turn off the beater bar on your vacuum.

## Can Area and Oriental Rugs Be Repaired?
Area and Oriental rugs can be repaired, but because they are often hand knotted, it is usually best to have a professional company repair them for you. Without the right knowledge, expertise, and equipment, you will likely do more damage to your rugs if you try to repair them yourself.

Oriental and area rugs should not be machine cleaned. Instead, they should be washed by hand only. If you choose to have your area rug cleaned with a machine, this will significantly diminish its overall value. The main reason that area rugs usually require repair work is due to heavy amounts of traffic which cause wear and tear to the corners and edges of the rugs; this referred to as overcasting, also known as serging. Other types of area rug repair services that are commonly needed include fringe restoration and the repairing of any holes.

## How Can You Ascertain The Value Of An Oriental Rug?

A certified rug cleaner can help you ascertain the value your area rug. The cleaner will work alongside a reputable appraiser to make sure the appraisal process is conducted properly, which ensures the full value of your rug is accurately calculated. A professional rug cleaner and appraiser will know all about the process of appraising rugs, including evaluating their origins, designs, types of knots used, and how they are sewn into the rug. Looking at both the front and back of the rug, an appraisal can be developed. Remember, if you are purchasing insurance for your rug -- and you should -- then you will need the value of the rug to be appraised.

Many factors play a part in ascertaining how much your oriental rug is worth. We could spend days talking about these different elements because Oriental rugs come in so many shapes, designs, and sizes. Though, the following factors are what a professional rug company will use to determine how much your oriental rug is worth:

- Materials used to make the rug
- Age
- Knot density
- Condition of the rug
- Design elements
- Demand and availability
- Colors
- Blending techniques
- Dye types

## What Area Rugs Cannot Be Cleaned With Water?

Rugs are made out of yarn. However, the exact type of yarn can vary. Some yarns are synthetic, whereas others are natural. The types of yarns used to make an area rug will influence the type of cleaning process the rug will need to undergo. Yarn that has colorfast dyes in it means "the color is in a condition that it will not run, bleed, or bleach." With this in mind, if you have a rug that is made of yarn that has non-colorfast dyes in it and water is introduced in the cleaning process, this means the colors can bleed and leak into one another, causing the rug to become damaged in relation to its appearance. Navajo area rugs are made of yarns that have not been pre-washed in an acidic solution, meaning they are not colorfast; because of this, they should not be cleaned with water.

## How Often Should Your Area Rug Be Professionally Cleaned?

An area rug or oriental rug should be professionally cleaned at least once every 18 to 24 months. Rugs that endure high amounts of traffic, however, should be cleaned even more frequently. Professional dust removal should be performed at least once a year on your rugs regardless of how much traffic they see. And remember, just because your rug does not look dirty does not mean it should not be cleaned. Regular cleaning is essential to extending the lifespan of your rug.

## What Is The Rug Cleaning Process?

There is much involved in cleaning an area or oriental rug. First of all, dust removal will take place in which a technician loosens any soil and removes it by performing an agitation process. Before this part of the cleaning process starts, though, the fibers and dyes will be tested to ensure the proper cleaning agents are used. Once the soil is loosened and removed, the rug will be rinsed, which helps to ensure any soils deeply embedded or entangled in the fibers are completely removed; while the rug is wet, a soft bristle agitator will be used to shampoo the rug. It depends on how soiled your rug is as to whether or not a rinsing and cleansing method needs to be performed more than once. However, once all centrifuge and extraction processes are performed, the rug will then be hung on a drying rack to allow for it to completely dry. There are essentially 14 steps involved in the rug cleaning process, but all 14 steps are not always needed. A professional rug cleaner can determine which exact steps are necessary according to your rug. For an overview of these 14 steps, visit Venturarugspa.com.

## What Should You Look For In Hiring A Professional Rug Cleaning Company?

Because area and oriental rugs are usually treasured, you will want to make sure they are cleaned professionally. Not only does this help the rugs to hold their value, but it also helps ensure their appearance is maintained to their sheer beauty. Hiring a professional rug cleaning company should be taken seriously, and you should make sure the company has lots of experience in cleaning rugs. You will want to check for references of the company to make sure their previous customers have been completely satisfied.

## Tips On Vacuuming Your Valuable Oriental Rug

Please keep in mind that many of today's standard vacuums are too aggressive for cleaning area rugs. If you have a wool area rug, you will want to clean it with a carpet sweeper rather than an electronic vacuum. If you do use a vacuum, make sure it's a canister vacuum and set the beater bar on it to put forth the least amount of abrasion as possible. Also, make sure you vacuum side to side rather than end to end; this helps ensure you don't grab the fringes of the rug. A handheld vacuum cleaner like a Miele is especially ideal for vacuuming area rugs; this type of vacuum doesn't have a roller bar.

Keeping your area and oriental rugs looking their best isn't difficult at all. You just need to make sure you clean them regularly, and when giving them a deep clean, let a professional cleaning company perform the involved processes for you. And always beware of the cleaning agents you are using on them to clean them, even if it's just water.

Section Six:

**Water Damage Restoration**

# Wet Carpets And Floors – Oh, My!

Water damage can lead to structural damage, musty odors, insect infestation, and many other costly outcomes. Sometimes, the results of water damage are not evident, such as when it leads to hardwood surface buckling. Nonetheless, though, it is imperative that the damages be resolved as soon as possible to help ensure no further damage occurs.

**What is Water Damage?**
Water damage can have detrimental effects not only on your residential or commercial property but your health as well if it is not dealt with properly, which is why it is so important to have the damage treated by a professional water damage restoration company. It is imperative to

understand that there are many types of water damage, meaning the exact type will determine the best restoration processes to carry out. A professional water damage restoration company can quickly evaluate the type of water damage that has occurred on your property followed by performing the most effective and efficient restoration methods.

Understanding what water damage is can be a bit complicated because there are so many various types. However, the best definition of water damage is damage that may be imperceptibly slow and minor such as water spots that could eventually mar a surface, or it may be instantaneous and catastrophic such as flooding. However fast it occurs, water damage is a major contributor to loss of property.

## How Water Damage Happens

Water damage can occur in multiple ways. From a broken toilet to torrential rain waters seeping in under your front door, any property is susceptible to water damage, making it crucial that you always have the number of a qualified water damage restoration company on hand at all times. Remember, the sooner water damage is assessed and repaired, the less costly it will be to perform the restoration services.

## Categories of Water Damage

As mentioned before, there are different classes of water damage, with each category having their restoration methods. Here's a quick overview of the three types of water damage.

**Category 1:** If water damage has occurred in a small amount, such as from a busted water pipe or a small amount of rain, it will fall under Category 1 Water Damage. Leaking appliances also generally lead to Category 1 water damage. The notable aspect of Category 1 Water Damage is that it is clean at its source, meaning it does not pose a hazard if it were to be consumed by people. This type of water damage does not require near as much time or equipment to remedy as the other two categories that we will discuss below. Other causes of Category 1 Water Damage also include melting snow or ice or a toilet bowl overflow.

**Category 2:** This type of water damage is commonly referred to as gray water, meaning it has some amount of contamination in it coming from the source of the damage. It is imperative to note that this type of water damage does present itself as moderately dangerous, and if consumed by people or animals, it has the potential of leading to sickness or discomfort. Common sources of Category 2 Water Damage are:

- Broken aquariums
- Washing machine overflow
- Punctured water beds
- Hydrostatic pressure seepage
- Toilet overflow with urine
- Discharge from dishwashers
- Sump pump back-up

All Category 2 Water Damage should be properly cleaned and treated within 48 hours, or it has the potential to evolve into Category 3 Water Damage. Common health effects that are possible due to exposure to Category 2 Water Damage include:

- Hypersensitivity pneumonitis (also known as lung tissue inflammation)
- Allergic rhinitis
- Burning eyes
- Allergic asthma
- Skin irritation
- Headache
- Inflammatory response
- Nausea
- and Fever

**Category 3:** Commonly referred to as black water, this type of water damage presents the most risk and danger. Water damage that has black water is highly contaminated, meaning it contains pathogens, which can lead to serious illness, and in some cases, it can even result in death. Those with a weak immune system which are exposed to Category 3 Water Damage should be kept away from the damaged premises at all times until the entirety of the damage has been assessed and thoroughly repaired. Causes of Category 3 Water Damage include:

- Ground surface water intrusion
- Flooding on the premises with the water source coming from a river or stream
- Toilet backflow from beyond the trap
- Sewage backup

Many adverse health effects can develop as a result of Category 3 Water Damage, with some of the most common being:

- Echovirus
- Parasites (Giardia/Cryptosporidium)
- Thermonospora
- Hepatitis

- E. coli
- Shigella
- Salmonella
- Rotavirus
- and Saccharopolyspora

All forms of Category 3 Water Damage should be dealt with immediately.

## The Process of Taking Care of Water Damage

No matter the category of water damage that occurs to your residential or commercial property, you should have it inspected and repaired as quickly as possible. Here is a quick overview of the process you should follow to take care of water damage.

**First**, you will need to contact an experienced clean-up company to inspect the damage. Any reputable company worth contacting will provide inspection services around the clock because they know that water damage can occur at any time and they understand the importance of having it inspected as quickly as possible to ensure the restoration process can start as soon as possible. There are six relevant pieces of information you should have when contacting a clean-up company to let them know about the water damage:

- Your name
- Address
- Insurance information
- Brief overview of damage
- The source of the damage (if you know)
- Whether or not electricity is available

**Next**, the clean-up company will arrive to perform an inspection. If the source of the water damage has not been stopped, the clean-up company will tackle this problem first, followed then by continuing the assessment of damage and creating a restoration plan. This restoration plan will involve removing and extracting any moisture, which may include the use of submersible pumps and industrial vacuum units depending on the extensiveness of the damage. The primary goal is to remove the water and moisture as quickly as possible to prevent further harm.

Because dampness will still be lingering after standing water has been removed, drying and dehumidifying is of the utmost importance in the restoration process. Industrial dehumidifiers are of extreme value, allowing for moisture to be removed so that it will not build up in porous building materials. The same industrial equipment can be used to dry carpet and various types of furniture.

**Lastly**, before final restoration can take place, your home and its furnishings will need to be sanitized once everything is completely dry. It is not uncommon for extreme dampness to leave behind various types of unpleasant odors, which makes the sanitization process all the more important. If needed, fogging equipment along with the help of industrial air scrubbers can be used to help eliminate problematic odors. Some cleanup companies will even go to the extent of using immersion cleaning and sanitizing equipment during the cleanup process.

**A basic overview of the restoration process is as follows:**

- Whatever is touched by black water is removed (drywall, baseboards, and hardwood floors get removed)

- The studs inside the walls and floors get dried out (even if it is concrete)

- Once dry, the floors get cleaned and treated with an antimicrobial & disinfectant to prevent mold and kill bacteria

## How Long Does it Take to Dry Out Your House?

If you are wondering how long it will take to dry out your house before water damage restoration can happen, you need to understand that no two cases of water damage are the same. Many factors will come into play in regards to exactly how long it takes for your home to dry. On average, though, a structure that has endured Category 1 Water Damage will take anywhere from three to five days to completely dry. Structures with Category 2 or Category 3 Water Damage take much longer to dry, often as long as two weeks.

## How to Go about Finding a Reputable Water Damage Restoration Company

There are several tips to keep in mind when it comes to finding a reputable water damage restoration company.

**First**, you will want to choose a company that has several years of experience in cleaning up water damage. The technicians working for this company should be industry certified and have plenty of references to back up their work. These recommendations should come from locals as well as trusted friends.

**Second**, you will also want to make sure the company has a rapid response rate to any questions you may have. After all, time is of great value when having water damage repaired.

**Third**, any company worth hiring will also be able to provide you with a detailed report of services they will be performing to make sure your water damage is repaired as swiftly and efficiently as possible. Along with this report, you will get a detailed quote of a price estimate. You may find some companies charge a flat rate fee for their services while others charge by the hour. Regardless of the way a company charges you, a detailed outline of the services you will be receiving and paying for should be provided to you.

Choosing a reputable water damage restoration company can save you tens of thousands of dollars in the long run. Not only will a reputable company be able to assess the damage to your property, but it will have access to the best equipment and supplies for repairing the damage as quickly as possible. Water damage can lead to very hazardous health concerns if not restored in the proper manner, so make sure you choose a company that has many years of experience and training in the water damage restoration field of work.

## Conclusion

Congratulations! You now have all of the information necessary to find a great carpet cleaning company. What's more, you have the ability to maintain your carpet and flooring between professional cleanings. Your carpets are an essential part of your decor - treat them as such. If you remember nothing else, make sure that you remember the following:

The Environmental Protection Agency (EPA) recommends cleaning your carpet at least once every 1-2 years, not only for aesthetic purposes but also for your health and hygiene. Keep in mind that your carpet will not always appear dirty to the naked eye. Tile is also incredibly important to clean on a regular basis. Bacteria and grime can quickly add up on tile, causing health issues and unsightly floor stains.

You can eliminate a significant amount of dirt from your carpeting by removing your shoes when you come into the house.

Keeping a clean carpet or flooring is essential if you are looking to sell your home in the immediate future. Flooring may be one of the last things that you look to as a resident, but it is one of the first things that will be checked out by potential buyers and real estate agents.

Make sure that any carpet cleaning company you hire is properly trained, educated and certified with accredited associations. Because of the highly unregulated nature of the carpet cleaning industry, supplement these certifications by making sure that your company comes to you highly recommended on review sites.

Looking at the cheapest company is usually a mistake. These companies simply will not be able to provide you with the level of expertise or the scale of technology that is needed to take care of any flooring problem. Investing in your flooring is investing in your home. Keeping your carpet clean pays back dividends well beyond the cost of a carpet cleaning. Price should never be your primary driver when choosing a company to clean your home.

Do not be afraid to ask a prospective carpet cleaning company the six critical questions that are listed in the chapter entitled "Buyer Beware: Bait & Switch Schemes and How to Avoid Them."

If it is time to replace your carpet or flooring, review the choices that are listed at the beginning of Section Three: "Your Carpet, Flooring, and Lifestyle." You have much more options than you may think.

Some commercially made carpet stain removers may make a stain worse! Pay close attention to your technique when applying DIY concepts for small spills. You can find some great tips in Section Four: "DIY Tips On Removing Spots, Spills, and Stains."

A wet vacuum can be your best friend, especially if you have pets or children who love to spill. If you do not have one in the home, make the small investment and learn how to use it. You will avoid many serious problems by stopping them in their tracks very early on.

If all else fails, call in the experts that you know you can trust ASAP. Timing is of the essence when it comes to your flooring. No matter how great your carpet cleaning company is, they can only do so much if you let a deep stain sit for hours or days!

This guide is meant to be used as an ongoing resource. We organized the topics in an intuitive way so that you can easily find what you are looking for regardless of the situation you are facing. Flooring emergencies happen quickly. Keep this guide close at hand so that you can handle spills as fast as possible.

Here's to getting and keeping more beautiful, healthy, long-lasting carpets and floors!

## About the Author

Smart Choice Cleaning is proud to be a local, independently owned and operated small business serving Northern Virginia and Washington, D.C.

Smart Choice Cleaning was founded in 2004 by John Alzubi, and the company has grown from a solo venture to a staff of more than 25 professionals focusing on hard work and a commitment to delivering exceptional service. John believes that "customer satisfaction" plays a huge part in establishing a rapport in business, and Smart Choice Cleaning has won multiple professional awards and designations.

Today, Smart Choice Cleaning is Northern Virginia's cleaning leader, offering residential and commercial cleaning solutions that include: routine maid services, specialty maid services, carpet and upholstery cleaning; tile and grout cleaning; and commercial janitorial services.

Our Mission:

"To provide the most outstanding customer experience ever!" You chose us, and we want you as a customer for life. We take pride in our highly-certified staff and top of the line equipment to give you a "clean like you have never seen." With Smart Choice Cleaning, you can feel confident that we will do our best to surpass your expectations.

What Sets Smart Choice Cleaning Apart?

Reputation: Smart Choice Cleaning is recognized for providing the most outstanding customer service in the area. Voted Best of NoVa 2015 in Northern Virginia Magazine and winner of Angie's List Super Service Awards for numerous years since 2010. We are also listed in the Best Pick Report in Fairfax, Arlington, Prince William and Loudoun County for 2011 through 2016 . We are a BBB member with an A+ rating and serve as the exclusive cleaning service for many Realtors, home contractors, and flooring retailers in the area.

Experience: Smart Choice Cleaning is experienced in both Residential and Commercial cleaning. We specialize in Carpet, Tile, Grout, and Upholstery Cleaning, Rug Cleaning, Maid and Janitorial Service, and Water Damage Restoration.

Systems: Smart Choice Cleaning uses the most advanced cleaning systems in the industry. We developed our own unique 12-step carpet cleaning process, using our truck-mounted cleaning equipment. We have a unique house cleaning process, proven to save our clients time and money. Our maids use our unique top-to-bottom, left-to-right, in-to-out, dry-to-wet cleaning method. We also use a comprehensive communication system that allows us to ensure accurately scheduled services.

Education: We believe that continuous education and training is key to ensuring the use of the latest techniques and following the highest quality standards for cleaning. All Smart Choice Cleaning field technicians attend weekly training sessions and in-house meetings. Smart Choice Carpet cleaning technicians are IICRC certified.

Guarantee: We offer a 100% money-back guarantee for our cleaning. If you are not completely satisfied, we will rush back at no charge to address your concerns. If you are still unsatisfied, we will honor our 100% money-back guarantee.

Made in the USA
Columbia, SC
21 June 2017